MW00576869

30 Marian Eucharistic Visits

Donna-Marie Cooper O'Boyle

Marian Eucharistic Visits

Adoring Jesus with His Mother

EWTN Publishing, Inc.
Irondale, Alabama

Copyright © 2023 by Donna-Marie Cooper O'Boyle

Printed in the United States of America. All rights reserved.

Cover design: LUCAS Art & Design, Jenison, MI.

Cover image: Madonna in the church Chiesa dei Santi Claudio
e Andrea dei Borgognoni by Guido Francisia (2043205607)
© Renata Sedmakova / Shutterstock.com.

Scripture quotations are taken from the New Revised Standard Version Bible: Catholic Edition, copyright © 1989, 1993 the Division of Christian Education of the National Council of the Churches of Christ in the United States of America. Used by permission. All rights reserved.

Excerpts from the English translation of the *Catechism of the Catholic Church* for use in the United States of America Copyright © 1994, United States Catholic Conference, Inc.—Libreria Editrice Vaticana. Used with Permission. English translation of the *Catechism of the Catholic Church: Modifications from the Editio Typica* copyright © 1997, United States Conference of Catholic Bishops—Libreria Editrice Vaticana.

No part of this book may be reproduced, stored in a retrieval system, or transmitted in any form, or by any means, electronic, mechanical, photocopying, or otherwise, without the prior written permission of the publisher, except by a reviewer, who may quote brief passages in a review.

EWTN Publishing, Inc.
5817 Old Leeds Road, Irondale, AL 35210

Distributed by Sophia Institute Press, Box 5284, Manchester, NH 03108.

paperback ISBN 978-1-68278-281-1

ebook ISBN 978-1-68278-282-8

Library of Congress Control Number: 2023939301

Second printing

Lovingly for my children: Justin, Chaldea,
Jessica, Joseph, and Mary-Catherine.
And much love for my grandchildren: Shepherd and Leo.

For Jesus and Mary: Forever I will give praise
to our Lord Jesus Christ, Bread of Life,
Savior of the World, and Lover of every soul.

I thank dear Mother Mary,
Our Lady of the Most Blessed Sacrament,
for being a Mother to me.

And I cannot forget dear St. Francisco Marto,
who often stole away to the tabernacle,
where he lovingly adored and consoled his "hidden Jesus."

Contents

Foreword

What a gem! What a treasure! What a pearl of infinite value! What a spiritual Marian masterpiece! I am referring to this Marian delight penned by the writer, speaker, author, and Marian lover Donna-Marie Cooper O'Boyle.

In these pages, Donna-Marie inspires us with a twofold spiritual blessing: (1) to visit the Eucharistic Heart of Jesus, truly present in every tabernacle, so as to better know, love, and worship the Lord of Lords and King of Kings; and (2) to make these Eucharistic visits in union with the mind, heart, and soul of Mary.

St. Louis de Montfort asserts that Mary is the quickest, shortest, and most efficacious pathway to Jesus. Our Lady said yes to God, and the Word became flesh and dwelt among us. Our Lady praised God in her Magnificat: "My soul magnifies the Lord, and my spirit rejoices in God my Savior." In these thirty Marian Eucharistic visits, you will learn, through the Immaculate Heart of Mary, to ponder the presence of Jesus, to talk heart-to-heart with Him, and to fall more in love with Him.

In Guadalupe, in Lourdes, and in Fátima, Our Lady asked for the same favor: to have a church built. The reason? So that all would be drawn magnetically to Jesus, present in the Most Holy Sacrament of the Altar, hidden as a Prisoner of love in the tabernacle.

In these visits to Jesus through the heart of Mary, you will also become familiar with some friends of Jesus and Mary. Pope St. John Paul II, St. Bernadette, St. Juan Diego, St. John Vianney, and many other saints will become your dear friends. Through their prayers, you will be drawn into deeper union with Jesus through Mary.

Donna-Marie's hope and desire is that all of us, from children to adults, will be drawn to Jesus through the Immaculate Heart of Mary, to adore our Eucharistic Lord, to repair for the sins against Him, to worship Him, and to supplicate and implore Him for countless graces.

Why not start today and continue every day for the next thirty days? Enter the church with your guardian angel and with Our Lady, queen of the angels and saints, and with this spiritual gem—*30 Marian Eucharistic Visits*. Genuflect before our Eucharistic Lord, and using *Lectio Divina*, read, ponder, and contemplate one Marian Eucharistic Visit per day. Then talk to Jesus and love Him through the most pure and Immaculate Heart of Mary.

The fruits of these thirty visits will be countless! Through the heart of Mary, you will know Jesus more, love Him more, converse with Him more, and imitate Him more by walking in His footsteps and in those of Mary. Finally, after knowing, loving, and imitating Jesus through Mary in this life, you will be welcomed by Jesus and Mary one day in Heaven. There with Mary, and the angels and saints, you will praise the Father, the Son, and the Holy Spirit for all eternity.

You have a gem in Donna-Marie's Marian Eucharistic masterpiece. Take this book as a friend before the Eucharistic Lord, share it with others, and then live out its simple but sublime message! May it transform your life now and for all eternity!

—Fr. Ed Broom, O.M.V., Oblates of the Virgin Mary

Preface

Draw near to God,
and He will draw near to you.

—James 4:8

I begin this labor of love on a special feast day. I decided to write this book a while back, and in God's timing, it is happening now. I am truly grateful that right now, amazingly in God's beautiful providence, the United States bishops have planned a Eucharistic Revival to span three years. Its aim is to inspire people to encounter Jesus Christ in the Eucharist. According to Pew Research, we are living in a time when only 31 percent of Catholics believe in the True Presence of Jesus in the Eucharist. Thus, the urgent need to do something to change those statistics.

As one of that 31 percent of believers, I wish to provide teaching and inspiration for you to take to your Eucharistic visits; for it was during time I spent with our dear Lord in Eucharistic Adoration that I received His unfathomable mercy, love, wisdom, and graces and where I grew closer to Him.

Our Lord calls us to keep Him company, to sit at His feet, to listen to His whispers to our soul. The night before His Crucifixion, Jesus asked Peter, James, and John to stay awake while He prayed in the garden. Jesus suffered greatly there. When He checked on His disciples, He asked Peter, "Couldn't you keep watch for one hour?" (see Mark 14:37).

The word *watch* is from the root Greek word *gregoreuo*, which means to pay special attention to avoid a catastrophic tragedy. The next line in Mark's Gospel speaks of praying to avoid temptation. Jesus knew prayer was necessary, especially at that time. He specifically asked His disciples to pray. They were tired after their leisurely Passover meal, however, and had trouble keeping their eyes open; and they fell asleep.

Let's ask our Mother Mary to help us stay awake; to help us to spend time with her Son; to help us to grow more in love with Him. St. Louis de Montfort stated, "It was through the Blessed Virgin Mary that Jesus came into the world, and it is also through her that He must reign in the world."[1] Jesus and Mary are truly inseparable. After all, it was inside her holy womb that Jesus spent His first nine months, rocked with her every move, nourished by her own body. It was at Mary's breasts where Baby Jesus was showered with love and tenderness and provided nourishment. On Mary's knee, Jesus learned His first prayers. His Mother's holy example as He grew helped to form His conscience, heart, and soul. Later, during His public ministry, Mary's continual earnest prayers and support aided Jesus in His mission to save mankind.

The Blessed Mother was an active co-redeemer with her Son, Jesus. She is still working hard from Heaven to save souls. Why should we not take Mary along with us when we go to spend

[1] St. Louis de Montfort, *True Devotion to the Blessed Virgin*, no. 1.

time with Jesus in the Blessed Sacrament? There is absolutely no reason not to! Mother Mary will always—and I mean *always*—lead us closer to her Son. Her loving wisdom will stir our hearts to a deeper devotion to Jesus.

Invite the Blessed Mother to accompany you on your visits with Jesus. She is very interested and attentive and will guide your prayers, gather them, perfect them, and offer them to her Son. Ask her to do this.

At times, you may be moved to tears in your prayers. Don't be afraid of your tears. Shed them freely while you are with Jesus. If possible, find times to visit Jesus when you can be alone with Him in your time of Adoration, wherever that might be. Pour your heart out to your Savior and beloved Friend.

30 Marian Eucharistic Visits: Adoring Jesus with His Mother is suitable for men and woman alike. I pray that this book will aid you on your journey. May God bless you in great abundance!

Yours in Jesus, Mary, and Joseph,

Donna-Marie Cooper O'Boyle
May 26, 2022
Feast of the Ascension of the Lord

Introduction

----

*I am the bread of life. Whoever comes to me will never be
hungry, and whoever believes in me will never be thirsty.*

—John 6:35

Our dear Lord Jesus Christ loves us so much that He makes Himself
present to us in an ordinary unpretentious piece of bread — a Host.
St. John Paul II said, "The Eucharist, in the Mass and outside of
the Mass, is the Body and Blood of Jesus Christ, and is therefore
deserving of the worship that is given to the living God, and to
Him alone."[2]

St. John Vianney, the Curé of Ars (1786–1859), who spent countless hours with Jesus in the Blessed Sacrament, passionately stated:

> Our Lord is hidden there in the tabernacle, waiting for us
> to come and visit Him, and make our requests to Him....

----

[2] Pope St. John Paul II, Opening Address in Ireland, Phoenix Park,
September 29, 1979.

1

In heaven, where we shall be glorious and triumphant, we shall see Him in all His glory. If He had presented Himself before us in that glory now, we should not have dared to approach Him; but He hides Himself like a person in prison, who might say to us, "You do not see Me, but that is no matter; ask of Me all you wish and I will grant it."

During his homilies, St. John Vianney often glanced at the tabernacle and passionately cried out, "He is there!"[3]

We know, without doubt, that our salvation comes through Jesus. Yet many of the saints have preached the necessity of getting to know the Blessed Virgin Mary so that she can bring us close to Jesus. Since the precise moment of the Annunciation, our Blessed Mother has cooperated with the Holy Spirit as she worked alongside her Son. She is our mighty intercessor and our loving advocate.

Remember, she said, "Do whatever He tells you" at the Wedding at Cana (John 2:5). She will always lead us to Jesus. She desires that all of mankind would "do whatever He tells you." She wants us all to be safe in Heaven one day.

Let us remember that it was Jesus Himself who gifted us with His Mother as He was dying on the Cross for our salvation. "Here is your mother," He told His disciple John (John 19:27). Mary then became the Mother of the Church. She is our true Mother!

The Marian saint Louis-Marie de Montfort has said that devotion to Mary is the surest, shortest, and most perfect way to

---

[3] John A. Hardon, S.J., *The History of Eucharistic Adoration: Development of Doctrine in the Catholic Church*, chap. 5, EWTN, https://www. ewtn.com/catholicism/library/history-of-eucharistic-adoration -development-of-doctrine-in-the-catholic-church-4086.

Introduction

approach Jesus. And Pope Pius XII, in his encyclical *Ad Caeli Reginam*, proclaims this:

> The Blessed Virgin possessed, after Christ, not only the highest degree of excellence and perfection, but also a share in that influence by which He, her Son and our Redeemer, is rightly said to reign over the minds and wills of men. For if through His Humanity the divine Word performs miracles and gives graces, if He uses His Sacraments and Saints as instruments for the salvation of men, why should He not make use of the role and work of His most holy Mother in imparting to us the fruits of redemption?[4]

Adoring our dear Lord is a beautiful form of prayer and a wonderful means to honor and praise Him. The *Catechism of the Catholic Church* (CCC) instructs us:

> *Adoration* is the first attitude of man acknowledging that he is a creature before his Creator. It exalts the greatness of the Lord who made us (cf. Ps. 95:1–6) and the almighty power of the Savior who sets us free from evil. Adoration is homage of the spirit to the "King of Glory" (Ps. 24:9–10), respectful silence in the presence of the "ever greater" God.[5] Adoration of the thrice-holy and sovereign God of love blends with humility and gives assurance to our supplications. (no. 2628).

Teachings and reflections (in the form of spiritual exercises) are provided in this book to accompany you on your visits to Jesus in

---

[4] Pope St. Pius XII, encyclical *Ad Caeli Reginam* (October 11, 1954), no. 42.
[5] Cf. St. Augustine, *En. in Ps.* 62,16: *PL* 36, 757–758.

3

the Blessed Sacrament. Even when you can't get to a church or a chapel—during a pandemic, when the church is locked, or when you cannot leave home due to illness or responsibility—you can still adore Our Lord. When St. Faustina and other saints couldn't get to a chapel, they adored Our Lord wherever they were. St. Faustina wrote in her *Diary*:

> I have come to know that Holy Communion remains in me until the next Holy Communion. A vivid and clearly felt presence of God continues in my soul.... My heart is a living tabernacle in which the living Host is reserved. I have never sought God in some far-off place, but within myself. It is in the depths of my own being that I commune with my God.[6]

Let us adore Our Lord as often as possible and ask Jesus' Mother, Mary, to accompany us!

---

[6] *Diary of Saint Maria Faustina Kowalska: Divine Mercy in My Soul* (Stockbridge, MA: Marians of the Immaculate Conception, 1981), no. 1302.

Prayer to Our Lady of the Most Blessed Sacrament

O Virgin Mary, Our Lady of the Most Blessed Sacrament, the glory of Christians, the joy of the universal Church, and the hope of the world, pray for us. Kindle in all the faithful a lively devotion to the most Holy Eucharist, so that they may all be made worthy to receive Holy Communion every day. Our Lady of the Most Blessed Sacrament, pray for us.

Let us with Mary Immaculate adore, thank, supplicate, and console the most sacred and beloved Eucharistic Heart of Jesus!

—St. Peter Julian Eymard

Practical Details

Each visit's spiritual exercise will include four elements: (1) *ponder* (usually a verse or quote), (2) *reflect* (a reflection or story), (3) *pray* (an inspiration and instructions for prayer), and (4) *savor* (an encouragement to rest in Our Lord's presence and even afterward to savor the graces and insights to ponder and pray over). In addition, there are spaces available to record your "lights, insights, and resolutions."

In essence, the spiritual exercises use a sort of *Lectio Divina* technique, but even if you are not familiar with *Lectio Divina*, you can easily take the suggested material to heart during your time with Jesus.

When you visit Jesus in the Blessed Sacrament, you can give thanks for the many blessings in your life, you can praise Our Lord, you can ask Him for something for yourself or others, and most importantly, you can seek His forgiveness for your shortcomings and sins.

You do not have to follow this book in chronological order. You may pick and choose which Marian Eucharistic visit (or reflection) or spiritual exercise to reflect upon during your time with Jesus in the Blessed Sacrament. You may also use the same spiritual exercises over and over again—no doubt, each time bringing new insights and lights.

I recommend that you jot down your thoughts or any insights you receive during or after your Eucharistic visits. The book will then become for you a unique spiritual journal that you can refer to any time. I also encourage you to make use of the meaningful prayers in the appendix.

St. John Vianney gives great advice for our Eucharistic visits. He said, "When we are before the Blessed Sacrament, instead of looking about us, let us shut our eyes and open our hearts; and the good God will open His. We will go to Him, and He will come to us, the one to give, and the other to receive. It will be like a breath passing from one to the other. What delight we find in forgetting ourselves that we may seek God."[7]

---

[7] St. John Vianney, "Catechism on the Real Presence," chap. 11 of *Catechetical Instructions*, Crossroads Initiative, https://www.crossroadsinitiative.com/media/articles/catechetical-instructions/.

Seeking the Conversion of Sinners with Mary

During this Eucharistic visit, pray for the conversion of sinners, as our Mother Mary has requested of us.

Ponder

O Most Holy Trinity, Father, Son, and Holy Spirit, I adore Thee profoundly. I offer Thee the most precious Body, Blood, Soul, and Divinity of Jesus Christ, present in all the tabernacles of the world, in reparation for the outrages, sacrileges, and indifferences by which He is offended. By the infinite merits of the Sacred Heart of Jesus and the Immaculate Heart of Mary, I beg the conversion of poor sinners.

—The Angel of Peace at Fátima, third apparition

Reflect

In 1916, in Fátima, Portugal, in a series of three apparitions, a radiant angel who had the appearance of a fourteen- or fifteen-year-old boy, visited three young shepherd children. He identified himself as the "Angel of Peace," and his purpose was to prepare the children's hearts for the Blessed Mother's apparitions, which would take place the following year.

Each time the angel visited them, the three visionaries—Lúcia, Francisco, and Jacinta—were very surprised, but they were completely at peace. During his visits, the angel invited the children to pray with him, and he told them, "The hearts of Jesus and Mary are attentive to the voice of your supplications."

The three young visionaries were filled with many graces, and their hearts were profoundly touched through praying with the Angel of Peace. The children began to pray more fervently and to make sacrifices for the conversion of sinners, as the angel had asked them.

On his third visit, the angel held a beautiful chalice in his left hand. God's abiding love enveloped the children, and they were fascinated to see a wondrous apparition unfold before them. A Eucharistic Host hovered above the chalice while drops of Jesus' Precious Blood dripped from the Host and fell into the chalice.

Suddenly, the Angel of Peace left the chalice and Host hovering miraculously in the air, and he knelt down to pray with the children. The radiant angel demonstrated to the children how they should worship God in Eucharistic Adoration. They all bowed down and touched their foreheads to the ground in reverent prayer to Jesus present in the Blessed Sacrament. The angel taught them the prayer that begins today's spiritual exercise. He asked them to pray it three times.

Pray

Put yourself in the presence of God. Invite the Blessed Mother to be with you in prayer.

Pray: Dear Jesus, Miracle of the Eucharist, thank You for the great gift of You! And thank You for allowing me to visit You now. Please forgive me for my sins and for any times I did not fully believe in Your presence in the Blessed Sacrament. Please stay with me.

Mother Mary, please assist me and help me to quiet my mind to focus on your Son, Jesus.

Spiritual Communion, Our Father, Hail Mary, Glory Be, and Prayer to Our Lady of the Most Blessed Sacrament.

Take a few moments to say the prayer of the Angel of Peace, slowly meditating upon the words. Pray the prayer three times slowly, earnestly beseeching the Holy Trinity, through the merits of the Sacred Heart of Jesus and the Immaculate Heart of Mary, to convert poor sinners.

Ask Jesus to speak to your heart. Be quiet and listen. If your mind wanders to other things, bring it back by asking Jesus and Mary to help you focus on your prayers. Also ask your guardian angel to assist you.

Praise: O Sacrament Most Holy, O Sacrament Divine, all praise and all thanksgiving be every moment Thine!

Pray: Pray for me, O Virgin Immaculate, Our Lady of the Most Blessed Sacrament.

Savor

Rest in the presence of the Lord. Close your eyes and put yourself into the scene with the Angel of Peace and the three shepherd children. Stay for as long as you can to keep our Eucharistic Lord company, as your circumstances allow.

Even after you leave your time of Adoration to go on with your responsibilities, recall the scene of the Angel of Peace teaching Eucharistic Adoration to the three young shepherds. Continue to lift your heart to God and pray for the conversion of sinners, being mindful that Our Lady of Fátima told the shepherd children that many go to Hell because they have no one to pray for them. Allow your heart to be a living tabernacle and commune with Jesus throughout your day. Feel free to record your thoughts or experiences below.

Lights, insights, resolutions:

_____

_____

_____

_____

_____

_____

_____

_____

Praying for Gifts of the Spirit and for Humility Like Mary's

During this Eucharistic visit, strive to pray for the gifts of the Holy Spirit and for the virtue of humility.

Ponder

God the Holy Spirit entrusted his wondrous gifts to Mary, His faithful spouse, and chose her as the dispenser of all He possesses, so that she distributes all His gifts and graces to whom she wills, as much as she wills, how she wills, and when she wills. No heavenly gift is given to men which does not pass through her virginal hands. Such indeed is the will of God, who has decreed that we should have all things through Mary, so that, making herself poor and lowly, and hiding herself in the depths of nothingness during her whole life, she might be enriched, exalted, and honored by almighty God. Such are the views of the Church and the early Fathers.

—St. Louis de Montfort, *True Devotion to the Blessed Virgin*, no. 25

Reflect

The Blessed Virgin Mary has prayed for God's holy will ever since she was a young child, entering the temple for God's service at the tender age of three. She was always in tune with the promptings of the Holy Spirit and was formed by Him throughout her life. At the Annunciation, she answered the angel Gabriel with her Fiat and opened her heart wide to the overshadowing of the Holy Spirit to be gifted with the treasure of the Son of God to reside within her.

God saw fit that His Holy Mother would be entrusted with the astounding gifts of the Holy Spirit—and not only that, but to be the *dispenser* of the holy gifts. As the Marian St. Louis de Montfort expressed, she would become "the dispenser of all He [the Holy Spirit] possesses, so that she distributes all His gifts and graces to whom she wills, as much as she wills, how she wills, and when she wills."

Knowing that our Mother Mary dispenses these ineffable gifts, strive to beg her earnestly for them, according to God's holy will. In addition, while you are with our Eucharistic Lord, ask Mary to help you attain the necessary virtue of humility. Mary is honored by God for her most pure humility. St. Catherine of Siena stated, "So greatly did the virtue of humility please Him in Mary that He was constrained to give her the Word, His Only-Begotten Son, and she was the sweet mother who gave Him to us."[8]

Pray

Put yourself in the presence of God. Invite the Blessed Mother to be with you in prayer.

Pray: Dear Jesus, Miracle of the Eucharist, thank You for the great gift of You! And thank You for allowing me to visit

---

[8] Jonathan Marshall, ed., in *Readings in Church History* (Hiram, ME: Hubbard Hill Press, 2009), 220.

You now. Please forgive me for my sins and for any times I did not fully believe in Your presence in the Blessed Sacrament. Please stay with me.

Mother Mary, please show me how to pray, and help me to quiet my mind to focus on your Son, Jesus.

Spiritual Communion, Our Father, Hail Mary, Glory Be, and Prayer to Our Lady of the Most Blessed Sacrament.

Ask Mary to teach you humility, and if it is God's holy will, to dispense gifts to you from the Holy Spirit.

Pray the *Litany of Humility* (found in the appendix).

Ask Jesus to speak to your heart. Be quiet and listen. If your mind wanders to other things, bring it back by asking Jesus and Mary to help you focus on your prayers. Also ask your guardian angel to assist you.

Praise: O Sacrament Most Holy, O Sacrament Divine, all praise and all thanksgiving be every moment Thine!

Pray: Pray for me, O Virgin Immaculate, Our Lady of the Most Blessed Sacrament.

Savor

Rest in the presence of the Lord. Take a breath. Close your eyes and put yourself into the scene, envisioning Mary opening her heart to the Holy Spirit in prayer and dispensing gifts from the Holy Spirit.

Ask Jesus to touch your heart in a special way, according to His holy will. Express your love to Jesus. Stay for as long as you can to keep our Eucharistic Lord company, as your circumstances allow.

Even after you leave your time of Adoration to go on with your responsibilities, recall the scene of Mary praying and dispensing spiritual gifts. Thank her for taking care of you. Allow your heart to be a living tabernacle and commune with Jesus throughout your day. Feel free to record your thoughts or experiences below.

Lights, insights, resolutions:

_____

_____

_____

_____

_____

_____

_____

_____

_____

_____

Adoring the Sacred Heart of Jesus with Mary

During this Eucharistic visit, ardently strive
to adore the Sacred Heart of Jesus.

Ponder

*The Heart of Christ! His "Sacred Heart" has given men
everything: redemption, salvation, sanctification. St. Faustina
Kowalska saw coming from this Heart that was overflowing with
generous love, two rays of light which illuminated the world.*

—Pope St. John Paul II, Homily on Divine Mercy Sunday, 2001

Reflect

The *Catechism* teaches:

Jesus knew and loved us each and all during his life, his
agony and his Passion, and gave himself up for each one
of us: "The Son of God ... loved me and gave Himself for
me" (Gal. 2:20). He has loved us all with a human heart.
For this reason, the Sacred Heart of Jesus, pierced by our
sins and for our salvation (cf. John 19:34), "is quite rightly
considered the chief sign and symbol of that ... love with

which the divine Redeemer continually loves the eternal Father and all human beings" without exception.[9] (478)

It's amazing to ponder the fact that Jesus has always known and has always loved each and every one of us. He suffered greatly for us to open wide the gates of Heaven for us. Yet we often doubt His great love; we sin, and we lose our way. Still, Our Lord Jesus is forever ready to swoop right in to scoop us up, draw us tight against His loving Sacred Heart, and forgive us. He wants us to turn from sin and to believe in His love and mercy.

One time, a sister in St. Faustina's religious order tearfully pleaded with the humble mystic to ask Jesus if her sins were forgiven and if her confessions were good enough. The desperate sister grasped Sr. Faustina's hand and wouldn't let go until her fellow sister agreed to do so. That evening, when Sr. Faustina asked Jesus in prayer about this sister, He told her to tell the sister that her disbelief wounded His Heart much more than the sins she had committed.[10]

Pray

Put yourself in the presence of God. Invite the Blessed Mother to be with you in prayer.

Pray: Dear Jesus, Miracle of the Eucharist, thank You for the great gift of You! And thank You for allowing me to visit You now. Please forgive me for my sins and for any times I did not fully believe in Your presence in the Blessed Sacrament. Please stay with me.

---

[9] Pope Pius XII, encyclical *Haurietis aquas* (1956): DS 3924; cf. DS 3812.

[10] St. Maria Faustina Kowalska, *Diary*, 628.

Mother Mary, please help me to quiet my mind to focus on your Son, Jesus, and please stay with me.

Spiritual Communion, Our Father, Hail Mary, Glory Be, and Prayer to Our Lady of the Most Blessed Sacrament.

Ponder the reflection above about Jesus's great love and mercy for you. Ask God to forgive you your sins and draw you to His Sacred Heart.

Pray the prayer to the Sacred Heart.

Prayer to the Sacred Heart
(From the Raccolta)

O Most Sacred Heart of Jesus, pour down Thy blessings abundantly upon Thy Church, upon the Supreme Pontiff, and upon all the clergy; give perseverance to the just; convert sinners; enlighten unbelievers; bless our parents, friends, and benefactors; help the dying; free the souls in Purgatory; and extend over all hearts the sweet empire of Thy love. Amen.

Ask Jesus to speak to your heart. Be quiet and listen. If your mind wanders to other things, bring it back by asking Jesus and Mary to help you focus on your prayers. Also ask your guardian angel to assist you.

Praise: O Sacrament Most Holy, O Sacrament Divine, all praise and all thanksgiving be every moment Thine!

Pray: Pray for me, O Virgin Immaculate, Our Lady of the Most Blessed Sacrament.

Savor

Rest in the presence of the Lord. Close your eyes and put yourself into the scene with Jesus' Heart "overflowing with generous love" and the "two rays of light which illuminated the world," which St. Faustina was privileged to see.

Ask Jesus to touch your heart in a special way, according to His holy will. Express your love to Jesus. Stay for as long as you can to keep our Eucharistic Lord company, as your circumstances allow.

Even after you leave your time of Adoration to go on with your responsibilities, recall the scenes and sentiments of your prayer time and any insights you might have gained. Allow your heart to be a living tabernacle and commune with Jesus throughout your day. Feel free to record your thoughts and experiences below.

Lights, insights, resolutions:

_____

_____

_____

_____

_____

_____

4

Making Reparation to Jesus' Sacred Heart with Mary

During this Eucharistic visit, strive to make reparation to Jesus' Sacred Heart.

Ponder

When I become immersed in the Lord's Passion, I often see the Lord Jesus, during adoration, in this manner: after the scourging, the torturers took the Lord and stripped Him of His own garment, which had already adhered to the wounds.

—St. Maria Faustina Kowalska, *Diary*, 408

Reflect

Our verse today is from St. Faustina's *Diary*. The humble mystic often meditated upon Our Lord's Passion. Jesus told Faustina that He is pleased when a soul meditates upon His sufferings and that in doing so, those souls will grow closer to Him and advance in the spiritual life.

St. Faustina recalled in her *Diary* what she saw during her meditation on the Lord's Passion. She wrote, "As they took [the Lord's garment] off, His wounds reopened; then they threw a dirty and tattered scarlet cloak over the fresh wounds of the Lord. The cloak, in some places, barely reached His knees." She was very specific.

> They made Him sit on a piece of beam. And then they wove a crown of thorns, which they put on His sacred head. They put a reed in His hand and made fun of Him, bowing to Him as to a king. Some spat in His face, while others took the reed and struck Him on the head with it. Others caused Him pain by slapping Him; still others covered His face and struck Him with their fists. Jesus bore all this with meekness. Who can comprehend Him—comprehend His suffering?

Can we even imagine what Jesus went through?

St. Faustina continued with the detail and a request:

> Jesus' eyes were downcast. I sensed what was happening in the most sweet Heart of Jesus at that time. Let every soul reflect on what Jesus was suffering at that moment. They tried to outdo each other in insulting the Lord. I reflected: Where does such malice in man come from? It is caused by sin. Love and sin have met. (408)

Pray

Put yourself in the presence of God. Invite the Blessed Mother to be with you in prayer.

Pray: Dear Jesus, Miracle of the Eucharist, thank You for the great gift of You! And thank You for allowing me to visit You now. Please forgive me for my sins and for any times I did not fully believe in Your presence in the Blessed Sacrament. Please stay with me.

Mother Mary, please open my heart to love your Son more and more, and help me to quiet my mind to focus on Jesus.

Spiritual Communion, Our Father, Hail Mary, Glory Be, and Prayer to Our Lady of the Most Blessed Sacrament.

Ask Jesus to speak to your heart. Be quiet and listen. If your mind wanders to other things, bring it back by asking Jesus and Mary to help you focus on your prayers. Also ask your guardian angel to assist you.

Praise: O Sacrament Most Holy, O Sacrament Divine, all praise and all thanksgiving be every moment Thine!

Pray: Pray for me, O Virgin Immaculate, Our Lady of the Most Blessed Sacrament.

Savor

Rest in the presence of the Lord. Close your eyes and put yourself into the scene with Jesus at the scourging at the pillar as St. Faustina described. Stay with Jesus; comfort Him. Ask Him to touch your heart in a special way, according to His holy will. Express your love to Jesus. Stay for as long as you can to keep our Eucharistic Lord company, as your circumstances allow.

Even after you leave your time of Adoration to go on with your responsibilities, recall the scenes and sentiments of your prayer time and any insights you might have gained. Allow your heart to be a living tabernacle and commune with Jesus throughout your day. Feel free to record your thoughts and experiences below.

30 Marian Eucharistic Visits

Lights, insights, resolutions:

_____

_____

_____

_____

_____

_____

_____

_____

_____

_____

_____

_____

_____

5

Trustful Surrender to God's Holy Will with Mary

During this Eucharistic visit, pray for the graces to seek a wholehearted surrender of God's holy will in your life.

Ponder

Then Mary said, "Here am I, the servant of the Lord; let it be with me according to your word."

—Luke 1:38

Reflect

We read in Scripture the account of our Mother Mary's yes to God's holy will:

> In the sixth month the angel Gabriel was sent by God to a town in Galilee called Nazareth, to a virgin engaged to a man whose name was Joseph, of the house of David. The virgin's name was Mary. And he came to her and said, "Greetings, favored one! The Lord is with you." But she was much perplexed by his words and pondered what sort of greeting this might be. The angel said to her, "Do

not be afraid, Mary, for you have found favor with God. And now, you will conceive in your womb and bear a Son, and you will name him Jesus. He will be great, and will be called the Son of the Most High, and the Lord God will give to him the throne of His ancestor David. He will reign over the house of Jacob forever, and of his kingdom there will be no end." Mary said to the angel, "How can this be, since I am a virgin?" The angel said to her, "The Holy Spirit will come upon you, and the power of the Most High will overshadow you; therefore the child to be born will be holy; he will be called Son of God. And now, your relative Elizabeth in her old age has also conceived a son; and this is the sixth month for her who was said to be barren. For nothing will be impossible with God." Then Mary said, "Here am I, the servant of the Lord; let it be with me according to your word." Then the angel departed from her. (Luke 1:26–38)

Mary's Fiat changed history. Thank God for Mary!

Pray

Put yourself in the presence of God. Invite the Blessed Mother to be with you in prayer.

Pray: Dear Jesus, Miracle of the Eucharist, thank You for the great gift of You! And thank You for allowing me to visit You now. Please forgive me for my sins and for any times I did not fully believe in Your presence in the Blessed Sacrament. Please stay with me.

Dear Mother Mary, thank you for your Fiat! Please help me to quiet my mind to focus on your Son, Jesus.

> *Spiritual Communion, Our Father, Hail Mary, Glory Be, and Prayer to Our Lady of the Most Blessed Sacrament.*

Read the Scripture passage above slowly and meditatively. Ask Jesus to speak to your heart. Be quiet and listen. If your mind wanders to other things, bring it back by asking Jesus and Mary to help you focus on your prayers. Also ask your guardian angel to assist you.

> *Praise:* O Sacrament Most Holy, O Sacrament Divine, all praise and all thanksgiving be every moment Thine!
>
> *Pray:* Pray for me, O Virgin Immaculate, Our Lady of the Most Blessed Sacrament.

Savor

Rest in the presence of the Lord. Close your eyes and put yourself into the scene with Mary and the angel Gabriel. Ask Mother Mary to assist you in your time with her Son. Ask her to grant you the graces to be better at accepting God's holy will in your life.

Ask Jesus to touch your heart in a special way, according to His holy will. Express your love to Jesus. Stay for as long as you can to keep our Eucharistic Lord company, as your circumstances allow.

Even after you leave your time of Adoration to go on with your responsibilities, recall the scenes and sentiments of your prayer time and any insights you might have gained. Allow your heart to be a living tabernacle and commune with Jesus throughout your day. Feel free to record your thoughts and experiences below.

30 Marian Eucharistic Visits

Lights, insights, resolutions:

_____

_____

_____

_____

_____

_____

_____

_____

_____

_____

_____

_____

6

Striving for a Generous Heart Like Mary

During this Eucharistic visit, pray for the graces to
become more generous like Mother Mary.

Ponder

*In those days Mary set out and went with haste to
a Judean town in the hill country, where she entered
the house of Zechariah and greeted Elizabeth.*

—Luke 1:39-40

Reflect

At the Annunciation, the angel Gabriel was sent to Mary to tell
her she was chosen to be the Mother of God and to inform her
about her cousin Elizabeth's miraculous pregnancy (after having
been barren). Mary was a very generous soul. The young Jewish
handmaiden chose to put her own needs aside to help her elderly
cousin Elizabeth. She could have stayed home with concerns for
herself, since she was newly pregnant and might have been trying to
grasp the meaning of carrying the Savior of the world in her womb.
In addition, she might have been wondering how her husband, St.

Joseph, would accept this sudden mysterious miracle. Still, Mary set out in haste and with great faith and love.

Upon entering Elizabeth's home, after traveling her hundred-mile journey, Mary greeted Elizabeth with a warm embrace. "When Elizabeth heard Mary's greeting, the child leaped in her womb. And Elizabeth was filled with the Holy Spirit and exclaimed with a loud cry, 'Blessed are you among women, and blessed is the fruit of your womb. And why has this happened to me, that the mother of my Lord comes to me?'" (Luke 1:41–43).

Mary was not looking for praise from Elizabeth. Filled with humility, Mary chose to speak of her "lowliness," giving glory to God instead. We can imagine this beautiful meeting of the cousins—both pregnant with new holy life—Jesus and John the Baptist. We can imagine the women's holy greeting and embrace and their blessed time together at Elizabeth and Zechariah's home.

Pray

Put yourself in the presence of God. Invite the Blessed Mother to be with you in prayer.

Pray: Dear Jesus, Miracle of the Eucharist, thank You for the great gift of You! And thank You for allowing me to visit You now. Please forgive me for my sins and for any times I did not fully believe in Your presence in the Blessed Sacrament. Please stay with me.

Dear Mother Mary, show me how to be humble and generous like you. Please help me to quiet my mind to focus on your Son, Jesus.

Spiritual Communion, Our Father, Hail Mary, Glory Be, and Prayer to Our Lady of the Most Blessed Sacrament.

Ask Jesus to speak to your heart. Be quiet and listen. If your mind wanders to other things, bring it back by asking Jesus and Mary to help you focus on your prayers. Also ask your guardian angel to assist you.

Praise: O Sacrament Most Holy, O Sacrament Divine, all praise and all thanksgiving be every moment Thine!

Pray: Pray for me, O Virgin Immaculate, Our Lady of the Most Blessed Sacrament.

Savor

Rest in the presence of the Lord. Close your eyes and put yourself into the scene with Mary and Elizabeth. In your imagination, watch them lovingly interact together.

Ask Jesus to touch your heart in a special way, according to His holy will. Express your love to Jesus. Stay for as long as you can to keep our Eucharistic Lord company, as your circumstances allow.

Even after you leave your time of Adoration to go on with your responsibilities, recall the scenes and sentiments of your prayer time and any insights you might have gained. Allow your heart to be a living tabernacle and commune with Jesus throughout your day. Feel free to record your thoughts and experiences below.

Lights, insights, resolutions:

_____

_____

_____

Acknowledging Christ's True Presence with Mary

During this Eucharistic visit, pray for the graces never to waver in your belief in Christ's True Presence in the Eucharist.

Ponder

May Mary, who in the freedom of her "Fiat" and her presence at the foot of the cross, offered to the world Jesus, the Liberator, help us to find Him in the Sacrament of the Altar.[11]

—Pope St. John Paul II

Reflect

Right from the start, Mother Mary was linked with her Son, Jesus, in the salvation of souls. Chosen by God, the Jewish teenaged Mary was visited by the angel Gabriel at the Annunciation. Mary consented to the gift of being chosen as the Mother of God and gave her Fiat. The first thirty years of Jesus' life were filled with

---

[11] "Quotes on the Most Blessed Sacrament," 6, Real Presence Eucharistic Education and Adoration Association, http://therealpresence.org/eucharst/tes/quotes6.html.

holy love and unending grace, intertwined with arduous struggles. No doubt, Mother Mary earnestly prayed all along. Later, Mary's prayers throughout Jesus' public ministry were meaningful and essential. Her instructions to the wine stewards at the wedding at Cana, "Do whatever He tells you," are words for us all.

Mary's presence at the foot of her Son's Cross speaks volumes to our weary hearts. She remains faithful and always shows us the way to her Son.

Pray

Put yourself in the presence of God. Invite the Blessed Mother to be with you in prayer.

Pray: Dear Jesus, Miracle of the Eucharist, thank You for the great gift of You! And thank You for allowing me to visit You now. Please forgive me for my sins and for any times I did not fully believe in Your presence in the Blessed Sacrament. Please stay with me.

Dear Mother Mary, teach me to be faithful and help me always to find your Son. Please help me to quiet my mind to focus on Jesus.

Spiritual Communion, Our Father, Hail Mary, Glory Be, and Prayer to Our Lady of the Most Blessed Sacrament.

Ask Jesus to speak to your heart. Be quiet and listen. If your mind wanders to other things, bring it back by asking Jesus and Mary to help you focus on your prayers. Also ask your guardian angel to assist you.

Praise: O Sacrament Most Holy, O Sacrament Divine, all praise and all thanksgiving be every moment Thine!

Pray: Pray for me, O Virgin Immaculate, Our Lady of the Most Blessed Sacrament.

Savor

Rest in the presence of the Lord. Close your eyes and put yourself into the scenes with Mother Mary as she gives her Fiat, raises the Child Jesus, prays for Him, and keeps a courageous, loving vigil at the foot of His Cross.

Ask Jesus to touch your heart in a special way, according to His holy will. Express your love to Jesus. Stay for as long as you can to keep our Eucharistic Lord company, as your circumstances allow.

Even after you leave your time of Adoration to go on with your responsibilities, recall the scenes and sentiments of your prayer time and any insights you might have gained. Allow your heart to be a living tabernacle and commune with Jesus throughout your day. Feel free to record your thoughts and experiences on the lines below.

Lights, insights, resolutions:

_____

_____

_____

_____

_____

_____

_____

_____

_____

_____

_____

_____

_____

_____

_____

_____

_____

_____

_____

8

Learning from Our Lady of Guadalupe

During this Eucharistic visit, pray for the graces
you need to be faithful to God's holy will.

Ponder

*Let not your heart be disturbed. Do not fear that sickness,
nor any other sickness or anguish. Am I not here, who is your
Mother? Are you not under my protection? Am I not your
health? Are you not happily within my fold? What else do
you wish? Do not grieve nor be disturbed by anything.* [12]

—Our Lady of Guadalupe to St. Juan Diego

Reflect

In 1531, Our Lady of Guadalupe appeared on the Hill of Tepeyac
in Mexico to a humble Native American named Juan Diego. The
mysterious visitor identified herself as "the ever-virgin Holy Mary,
Mother of the true God for whom we live, of the Creator of all
things, Lord of Heaven and earth." She requested that a chapel be

---

[12] "Our Lady of Guadalupe," Catholic News Agency, https://www.
catholicnewsagency.com/resource/55425/our-lady-of-guadalupe.

built in her honor. Our Lady sent Juan Diego to the bishop with this request, and the bishop asked for a sign.

In following Our Lady's instructions to pick roses to bring to the bishop, Juan Diego discovered beautiful roses miraculously growing in December atop a high hill. In addition to the roses, Our Lady of Guadalupe left for us a miraculous image of herself imprinted on Juan Diego's tilma. This tilma, which was a poor-quality cactus cloth, should have deteriorated within about twenty years. However, 476 years later, it still shows no sign of decay, and the image on it completely defies all scientific explanations of its origin. Studies show that reflected in Our Lady's eyes in the image is what was in front of her when she appeared in 1531.

Pray

Put yourself in the presence of God. Invite the Blessed Mother to be with you in prayer.

Pray: Dear Jesus, Miracle of the Eucharist, thank You for the great gift of You! And thank You for allowing me to visit You now. Please forgive me for my sins and for any times I did not fully believe in Your presence in the Blessed Sacrament. Please stay with me.

Our Lady of Guadalupe, please pray for me and help me to quiet my mind to focus on your Son Jesus.

Spiritual Communion, Our Father, Hail Mary, Glory Be, and Prayer to Our Lady of the Most Blessed Sacrament.

Ask Jesus to speak to your heart. Be quiet and listen. If your mind wanders to other things, bring it back by asking Jesus and Mary to help you focus on your prayers. Also ask your guardian angel to assist you.

Praise: O Sacrament Most Holy, O Sacrament Divine, all praise and all thanksgiving be every moment Thine!

Pray: Pray for me, O Virgin Immaculate, Our Lady of the Most Blessed Sacrament.

Savor

Rest in the presence of the Lord. Close your eyes and put yourself into the scene with Our Lady of Guadalupe and St. Juan Diego.

Ask Jesus to touch your heart in a special way, according to His holy will. Express your love to Jesus. Stay for as long as you can to keep our Eucharistic Lord company, as your circumstances allow.

Even after you leave your time of Adoration to go on with your responsibilities, recall the scenes and sentiments of your prayer time and any insights you might have gained. Allow your heart to be a living tabernacle and commune with Jesus throughout your day. Feel free to record your thoughts and experiences below.

Lights, insights, resolutions:

_____

_____

_____

_____

_____

_____

_____

_____

_____

_____

_____

_____

_____

_____

_____

_____

_____

_____

_____

_____

_____

9

Learning from Our Lady of Fátima

During this Eucharistic visit, pray for the graces to be open to enduring any sufferings Our Lord allows for you for reparation and for the conversion of sinners.

Ponder

Do you wish to offer yourselves to God to endure all the sufferings that He may be pleased to send you, as both an act of reparation for the sins with which He is offended and an act of supplication for the conversion of sinners?

—Our Lady of Fátima to the shepherd children

Reflect

On May 13, 1917, Our Lady of Fátima appeared to three young shepherd children in Fátima, Portugal. It would be the first of her six visits to that area. These apparitions were preceded by visits in 1916 from the Angel of Peace, who prepared the children for the Blessed Mother's visits and instructions (see Marian Eucharistic Visit 1). The message of Fátima calls us to turn away from sin, pray the Rosary daily for peace in the world, and offer penance for sinners.

St. John Paul II claimed Fátima was the greatest apparition of the twentieth century and possibly of all time. Fátima expert Fr. Andrew Apostoli, C.F.R., stated that Our Lady of Fátima's message is even more relevant today than in 1917. He said that she calls her children to lead holy lives of prayer and penance. Fr. Apostoli noted that many people reject sacrifice because they are too attached to worldly and sinful things. He claimed if we follow what Our Lady asks, however, we will come closer to Jesus.[13]

Pray

Put yourself in the presence of God. Invite the Blessed Mother to be with you in prayer.

Pray: Dear Jesus, Miracle of the Eucharist, thank You for the great gift of You! And thank You for allowing me to visit You now. Please forgive me for my sins and for any times I did not fully believe in Your presence in the Blessed Sacrament. Please stay with me.

Our Lady of Fátima, please teach me your ways, and help me to quiet my mind to focus on your Son, Jesus.

Spiritual Communion, Our Father, Hail Mary, Glory Be, and Prayer to Our Lady of the Most Blessed Sacrament.

Ask Jesus to speak to your heart. Be quiet and listen. If your mind wanders to other things, bring it back by asking Jesus and Mary to help you focus on your prayers. Also ask your guardian angel to assist you.

---

[13] Donna-Marie Cooper O'Boyle, *Our Lady of Fatima: 100 Years of Stories, Prayers, and Devotions* (Cincinnati: Servant, 2017), 10.

Praise: O Sacrament Most Holy, O Sacrament Divine, all praise and all thanksgiving be every moment Thine!

Pray: Pray for me, O Virgin Immaculate, Our Lady of the Most Blessed Sacrament.

Savor

Rest in the presence of the Lord. Close your eyes and put yourself into the scene with Our Lady of Fátima and the shepherd children.

Ask Jesus to touch your heart in a special way, according to His holy will. Express your love to Jesus. Stay for as long as you can to keep our Eucharistic Lord company, as your circumstances allow.

Even after you leave your time of Adoration to go on with your responsibilities, recall the scenes and sentiments of your prayer time and any insights you might have gained. Allow your heart to be a living tabernacle and commune with Jesus throughout your day. Feel free to record your thoughts and experiences below.

Lights, insights, resolutions:

_____

_____

_____

_____

_____

_____

30 Marian Eucharistic Visits

_____

_____

_____

_____

_____

_____

_____

_____

_____

_____

_____

_____

_____

10

Learning from Our Lady of Lourdes

During this Eucharistic visit, pray for the graces to view
each day of life as another opportunity to obey the
commandments, do good, and grow closer to God.

Ponder

I do not promise you happiness in this world but in the next.

—Our Lady of Lourdes to St. Bernadette

Reflect

On February 11, 1858, fourteen-year-old Bernadette Soubirous,
a French peasant girl, was visited by a mysterious and beautiful
woman dressed in a dazzling white dress with a blue sash around
her waist. It was the first of eighteen visits. Bernadette had been
gathering firewood near a stone grotto when she became completely
mesmerized by the sudden appearance of the beautiful Lady. The
Lady would later identify herself to Bernadette on March 25, 1858,
when she told the peasant girl, "I am the Immaculate Conception."

Pope Benedict XVI said, "In Lourdes, the Holy Virgin invites all to regard earth as a place of pilgrimage toward our final

homeland, which is heaven. In reality, we are all pilgrims, we need Mary to guide us; and in Lourdes, her smile invites us to go forward with great confidence in the awareness that God is good, God is love."[14]

St. Bernadette's final words before leaving this earthly pilgrimage were: "Holy Mary, Mother of God, pray for me, a poor sinner."

Pray

Put yourself in the presence of God. Invite the Blessed Mother to be with you in prayer.

Pray: Dear Jesus, Miracle of the Eucharist, thank You for the great gift of You! And thank You for allowing me to visit You now. Please forgive me for my sins and for any times I did not fully believe in Your presence in the Blessed Sacrament. Please stay with me.

Holy Mary, Mother of God, Our Lady of Lourdes, pray for me, a poor sinner, and guide me and all pilgrims to Heaven. Please help me to quiet my mind to focus on your Son, Jesus.

Spiritual Communion, Our Father, Hail Mary, Glory Be, and Prayer to Our Lady of the Most Blessed Sacrament.

Ask Jesus to speak to your heart. Be quiet and listen. If your mind wanders to other things, bring it back by asking Jesus and Mary to help you focus on your prayers. Also ask your guardian angel to assist you.

[14] Pope Benedict XVI, General Audience, September 17, 2008, speaking of his September 12–15 apostolic trip to Paris and Lourdes.

Praise: O Sacrament Most Holy, O Sacrament Divine, all praise and all thanksgiving be every moment Thine!

Pray: Pray for me, O Virgin Immaculate, Our Lady of the Most Blessed Sacrament.

Savor

Rest in the presence of the Lord. Close your eyes and put yourself into the scene with Our Lady and St. Bernadette at the Grotto of Lourdes.

Ask Jesus to touch your heart in a special way, according to His holy will. Express your love to Jesus. Stay for as long as you can to keep our Eucharistic Lord company, as your circumstances allow.

Even after you leave your time of Adoration to go on with your responsibilities, recall the scenes and sentiments of your prayer time and any insights you might have gained. Allow your heart to be a living tabernacle and commune with Jesus throughout your day. Feel free to record your thoughts and experiences below.

Lights, insights, resolutions:

_____

_____

_____

_____

_____

11

Running in Haste with Mary

During this Eucharistic visit, pray to be a brilliant
light of faith, hope, and love when helping others.

Ponder

Do whatever He tells you.

—John 2:5

Reflect

The Blessed Mother was undoubtably a bright beacon of faith,
hope, and love to others—first, within her own humble home in
Nazareth and also as she reached out to others in various circumstances. Certainly, we are inspired by Mary's selfless generosity as
she ran in haste to help her older cousin St. Elizabeth. We meditate
upon Mary's loving heart when we pray the Second Joyful Mystery
of the Holy Rosary—the Visitation. In addition to Mary's famous
journey and her subsequent visit with St. Elizabeth, we see that she
was quick to reach out in love and care to all needs that presented
themselves. Her quick sizing up of a young newly married couple's
dilemma—having run out of wine for their guests—saved the day

and revealed to us her loving, generous heart. At the wedding at Cana, Mary told the wine stewards, in reference to Jesus, "Do whatever He tells you."

After Jesus' Ascension, Mary joined His disciples and stayed with them in the Upper Room, allaying their fears and waiting for the coming of the Holy Spirit. Her life was overflowing with kindness and loving compassion. With Mary's help, we can aspire to emulate her beautiful virtues as we strive to come closer to her Son.

Pray

Put yourself in the presence of God. Invite the Blessed Mother to be with you in prayer.

Pray: Dear Jesus, Miracle of the Eucharist, thank You for the great gift of You! And thank You for allowing me to visit You now. Please forgive me for my sins and for any times I did not fully believe in Your presence in the Blessed Sacrament. Please stay with me.

Mother Mary, please allay my fears and help me to quiet my mind to focus on your Son, Jesus.

Spiritual Communion, Our Father, Hail Mary, Glory Be, and Prayer to Our Lady of the Most Blessed Sacrament.

Ask Jesus to speak to your heart. Be quiet and listen. If your mind wanders to other things, bring it back by asking Jesus and Mary to help you focus on your prayers. Also ask your guardian angel to assist you.

Praise: O Sacrament Most Holy, O Sacrament Divine, all praise and all thanksgiving be every moment Thine!

Pray: Pray for me, O Virgin Immaculate, Our Lady of the Most Blessed Sacrament.

Savor

Rest in the presence of the Lord. Close your eyes and put yourself into the scene with the Blessed Mother doling out love and kindness to others within any of the events described above. Allow Mary to draw you closer to her Son so that you may always "do whatever He tells you."

Ask Jesus to touch your heart in a special way, according to His holy will. Express your love to Jesus. Stay for as long as you can to keep our Eucharistic Lord company, as your circumstances allow.

Even after you leave your time of Adoration to go on with your responsibilities, recall the scenes and sentiments of your prayer time and any insights you might have gained. Allow your heart to be a living tabernacle and commune with Jesus throughout your day. Feel free to record your thoughts and experiences below.

Lights, insights, resolutions:

_____

_____

_____

_____

_____

_____

_____

_____

_____

_____

_____

_____

_____

_____

_____

_____

_____

_____

_____

12

At the Foot of the Cross with Mary

During this Eucharistic visit, pray for the graces
to accompany Mother Mary standing
at the foot of Jesus' Cross.

Ponder

*Meanwhile, standing near the cross of Jesus were his mother,
and his mother's sister, Mary the wife of Clopas, and Mary
Magdalene. When Jesus saw his mother and the disciple whom
he loved standing beside her, he said to his mother, "Woman, here
is your son." Then he said to the disciple, "Here is your mother."
And from that hour the disciple took her into his own home.*

—John 19:25–27

Reflect

Mother Mary never gave up. She has always been united to her
Son and His mission, from the very moment of the Annuncia-
tion, and she stayed by Him throughout His Passion and beyond.
We will never fully understand the unspeakable sorrow that filled
Mother Mary's heart to overflowing as she stood and watched
her Son hanging, nailed to the Cross. Her ears listened to His

heart-wrenching words and His sighs. Her grieving, tear-filled eyes sorely witnessed every drop of His precious Blood being shed for our salvation.

Mary stood at the foot of the Cross as Jesus' Mother and also as His follower, and there she became our loving Mother in that eminent moment when Jesus gave His disciple John—and all disciples until the end of time—the illustrious gift of His own sweet Mother. Mary's great faith, love, and perseverance help to mold our own hearts and consciences. We must remember that she is our true Mother and is always there for us, guiding us to our true home in Heaven.

Pray

Put yourself in the presence of God. Invite the Blessed Mother to be with you in prayer.

Pray: Dear Jesus, Miracle of the Eucharist, thank You for the great gift of You! And thank You for allowing me to visit You now. Please forgive me for my sins and for any times I did not fully believe in Your presence in the Blessed Sacrament. Please stay with me.

Mother Mary, please show me the way to your Son every day. Help me to quiet my mind to focus on Jesus.

Spiritual Communion, Our Father, Hail Mary, Glory Be, and Prayer to Our Lady of the Most Blessed Sacrament.

Ask Jesus to speak to your heart. Be quiet and listen. If your mind wanders to other things, bring it back by asking Jesus and Mary to help you focus on your prayers. Also ask your guardian angel to assist you.

Praise: O Sacrament Most Holy, O Sacrament Divine, all praise and all thanksgiving be every moment Thine!

Pray: Pray for me, O Virgin Immaculate, Our Lady of the Most Blessed Sacrament.

Savor

Rest in the presence of the Lord. Close your eyes and put yourself into the scene with Mother Mary standing courageously and sorrowfully at the foot of her Son's Cross.

Ask Jesus to touch your heart in a special way, according to His holy will. Express your love to Jesus. Stay for as long as you can to keep our Eucharistic Lord company, as your circumstances allow.

Even after you leave your time of Adoration to go on with your responsibilities, recall the scenes and sentiments of your prayer time and any insights you might have gained. Allow your heart to be a living tabernacle and commune with Jesus throughout your day. Feel free to record your thoughts and experiences below.

Lights, insights, resolutions:

_____

_____

_____

_____

_____

_____

_____

_____

_____

_____

_____

_____

_____

_____

_____

_____

_____

13

Becoming a Handmaid or Servant with Mary

During this Eucharistic visit, pray for the graces to
emulate Mary's readiness to serve the Lord and others.

Ponder

Thus all things happened as arranged by the Mother of humility
and she obeyed as a handmaid. Laying aside all pretense
to her dignity as Queen and Lady, and making no use of
her sovereignty and dominion, she obeyed as a servant and
conducted herself as if she were an inferior, and in this spirit.

—Venerable Mary of Jesus of Ágreda, *Mystical City of God* 4, 48

Reflect

Even though Mary is the Mother of God and the Queen of
Heaven and earth, she always comported herself and acted in
deep humility during her life on earth. She consistently sought to
be of service to others. Venerable Mary of Ágreda, who was said
to have received visits from the Blessed Mother, kept a journal
of their conversations. They are collected in the book *Mystical
City of God*. Mary of Ágreda said that she observed Mary during

her visit to her cousin St. Elizabeth. She recalled that Mary was quick to pick up a dust cloth or a broom to humbly help clean St. Elizabeth's home.

Our Blessed Mother gives us a beautiful example of service to others with the deepest humility. The devil hates humility and does not know how to deal with it. Humility thwarts the evil one's tricks. Yet that is not the reason the Mother of God chooses the lowly tasks and always operates through humility. She does so in order to praise, honor, and glorify her Son's unequaled humility. Mary's thoughts, words, and actions and her entire being seek to glorify God.

Pray

Put yourself in the presence of God. Invite the Blessed Mother to be with you in prayer.

Pray: Dear Jesus, Miracle of the Eucharist, thank You for the great gift of You! And thank You for allowing me to visit You now. Please forgive me for my sins and for any times I did not fully believe in Your presence in the Blessed Sacrament. Please stay with me.

Dear Mother Mary, help me to become humble. Please help me to quiet my mind to focus on your Son, Jesus.

Spiritual Communion, Our Father, Hail Mary, Glory Be, and Prayer to Our Lady of the Most Blessed Sacrament.

Ask Jesus to speak to your heart. Be quiet and listen. If your mind wanders to other things, bring it back by asking Jesus and Mary to help you focus on your prayers. Also ask your guardian angel to assist you.

Praise: O Sacrament Most Holy, O Sacrament Divine, all praise and all thanksgiving be every moment Thine!

Pray: Pray for me, O Virgin Immaculate, Our Lady of the Most Blessed Sacrament.

Savor

Rest in the presence of the Lord. Close your eyes and put yourself into the scene with our Blessed Mother mopping the floor in St. John the apostle's home or dusting the furniture in St. Elizabeth's home.

Ask Jesus to touch your heart in a special way, according to His holy will. Express your love to Jesus. Stay for as long as you can to keep our Eucharistic Lord company, as your circumstances allow.

Even after you leave your time of Adoration to go on with your responsibilities, recall the scenes and sentiments of your prayer time and any insights you might have gained. Allow your heart to be a living tabernacle and commune with Jesus throughout your day. Feel free to record your thoughts and experiences below.

Lights, insights, resolutions:

_____

_____

_____

_____

_____

14

Giving Up Fear with Mary

During this Eucharistic visit, pray for the graces
to completely turn your fears over to God.

Ponder

*The angel said to her, "Do not be afraid, Mary, for you have
found favor with God. And now, you will conceive in your
womb and bear a Son, and you will name Him Jesus."*

—Luke 1:30-31

Reflect

How many times might the angel Gabriel have instructed people
not to be afraid? We know through Scripture that Gabriel told
the Blessed Mother, "Do not be afraid, Mary," when he appeared
to her at the Annunciation. Gabriel might have startled Mary
with his sudden appearance and wanted to put her at ease. Mary
was not afraid of the angel but was perplexed at his message.
The angel knew God was entrusting something quite huge to
the Jewish teen. Therefore, his instruction not to be afraid was
very appropriate.

Let's consider other times in Mary's life when there was reason to fear, such as not knowing where her precious Son would be born when she and St. Joseph struggled to find a place to stay in Bethlehem. We can be sure that Mary and St. Joseph were quite concerned to have to flee suddenly to Egypt to protect the infant Jesus from Herod. In addition, it must have been a terrible time of distress for the holy couple when Jesus was left behind in the temple and lost to them for three days. Undoubtably in each of these cases, Mary trusted her Father in Heaven and gave all her fear to Him.

Pray

Put yourself in the presence of God. Invite the Blessed Mother to be with you in prayer.

Pray: Dear Jesus, Miracle of the Eucharist, thank You for the great gift of You! And thank You for allowing me to visit You now. Please forgive me for my sins and for any times I did not fully believe in Your presence in the Blessed Sacrament. Please stay with me.

Dear Mother Mary, help me to surrender my fears to your Son. Please help me to quiet my mind to focus on Jesus.

Spiritual Communion, Our Father, Hail Mary, Glory Be, and Prayer to Our Lady of the Most Blessed Sacrament.

Ask Jesus to speak to your heart. Be quiet and listen. If your mind wanders to other things, bring it back by asking Jesus and Mary to help you focus on your prayers. Also ask your guardian angel to assist you.

Praise: O Sacrament Most Holy, O Sacrament Divine, all praise and all thanksgiving be every moment Thine!

Pray: Pray for me, O Virgin Immaculate, Our Lady of the Most Blessed Sacrament.

Savor

Rest in the presence of the Lord. Close your eyes and put yourself into one of the scenes in which Mary and Joseph experienced fear or anxiety.

Ask Jesus to touch your heart in a special way, according to His holy will. Express your love to Jesus. Stay for as long as you can to keep our Eucharistic Lord company, as your circumstances allow.

Even after you leave your time of Adoration to go on with your responsibilities, recall the scenes and sentiments of your prayer time and any insights you might have gained. Allow your heart to be a living tabernacle and commune with Jesus throughout your day. Feel free to record your thoughts and experiences below.

Lights, insights, resolutions:

_____

_____

_____

_____

_____

Saying Yes Like Mary

During this Eucharistic visit,
pray for the graces to answer yes to God.

Ponder

*Here am I, the servant of the Lord; let it be
with me according to your word.*

—Luke 1:38

Reflect

In his encyclical on the Blessed Mother, *Redemptoris Mater*, St. John Paul II told us:

> This fiat of Mary—"let it be to me"—was decisive, on the human level, for the accomplishment of the divine mystery. There is a complete harmony with the words of the Son, who, according to the Letter to the Hebrews, says to the Father as he comes into the world: "Sacrifices and offering you have not desired, but a body you have prepared for me.... Lo, I have come to do your will, O God" (Heb. 10:5-7). The mystery of the Incarnation was accomplished when Mary

uttered her fiat: "Let it be to me according to your word," which made possible, as far as it depended upon her in the divine plan, the granting of her Son's desire.[15]

Mary always wanted whatever her Son desired. Even before He was conceived by the Holy Spirit in her womb, she wholeheartedly desired God's holy will in her life. When she learned of Heaven's designs on her soul, she said, "Let it be with me according to your word." These courageous loving words would change the world forever.

We will never accomplish what the Mother of God has done for the world. Still, our own yes to God's holy will in small and big ways will change our own hearts and can help to change the hearts of others.

Pray

Put yourself in the presence of God. Invite the Blessed Mother to be with you in prayer.

Pray: Dear Jesus, Miracle of the Eucharist, thank You for the great gift of You! And thank You for allowing me to visit You now. Please forgive me for my sins and for any times I did not fully believe in Your presence in the Blessed Sacrament. Please stay with me.

Dear Mother Mary, teach me to say yes to God. Please help me to quiet my mind to focus on your Son, Jesus.

Spiritual Communion, Our Father, Hail Mary, Glory Be, and Prayer to Our Lady of the Most Blessed Sacrament.

[15] Pope St. John Paul II, encyclical *Redemptoris Mater* (March 24, 1987), no. 13.

Ask Jesus to speak to your heart. Be quiet and listen. If your mind wanders to other things, bring it back by asking Jesus and Mary to help you focus on your prayers. Also ask your guardian angel to assist you.

Praise: O Sacrament Most Holy, O Sacrament Divine, all praise and all thanksgiving be every moment Thine!

Pray: Pray for me, O Virgin Immaculate, Our Lady of the Most Blessed Sacrament.

Savor

Rest in the presence of the Lord. Close your eyes and put yourself into one of the scenes in which Mary said yes to God: her yes at the Annunciation, her yes in giving birth in a stable, her yes to staying with Jesus, at every precarious time, no matter what—even at the foot of the Cross.

Ask Jesus to touch your heart in a special way, according to His holy will. Express your love to Jesus. Stay for as long as you can to keep our Eucharistic Lord company, as your circumstances allow.

Even after you leave your time of Adoration to go on with your responsibilities, recall the scenes and sentiments of your prayer time and any insights you might have gained. Allow your heart to be a living tabernacle and commune with Jesus throughout your day. Feel free to record your thoughts and experiences below.

Lights, insights, resolutions:

_____

_____

_____

_____

_____

_____

_____

_____

_____

_____

_____

_____

_____

_____

_____

_____

16

Learning to Worship Like Mary

During this Eucharistic visit, pray for the graces to be more like beautiful Mary in worshipping Jesus.

Ponder

At Nazareth Joseph's days were filled with work . . . but when evening brought him home again, he would pass the entire night in adoration, never tiring, only too happy for the chance to contemplate the hidden riches of Jesus's divinity.[16]

—St. Peter Julian Eymard

Reflect

We will never be able to worship like Mary. Still, we can strive to learn from her and ask for her assistance. Stepping back to the beginning in Nazareth, we see that Mary's parents, St. Anne and St. Joachim, faithfully raised their daughter in their Jewish tradition, cultivating within her a pure love for God. Keeping their promise

[16] "Quotes on the Most Blessed Sacrament," 15, Real Presence Eucharistic Education and Adoration Association, http://therealpresence.org/eucharst/tes/quotes15.html.

to God for the miracle of conceiving Mary in barren St. Anne's womb, they dedicated their three-year-old daughter Mary to the temple, where she was taught by the masters.

Fast-forward now to grown Mary, married to St. Joseph, and with Jesus residing in her womb, being rocked by Mary's every move. Without a doubt, Mary and Joseph basked in the holiness of Jesus, always near them in their humble abode—worshipping Him in His first tabernacle: Mary's womb. We see that Mary's life was always steeped in fervent dedicated prayer and lively grace. She was Jesus' Holy Mother, but she also knew she was to worship her Son, Jesus. That she did so beautifully.

Pray

Put yourself in the presence of God. Invite the Blessed Mother to be with you in prayer.

Pray: Dear Jesus, Miracle of the Eucharist, thank You for the great gift of You! And thank You for allowing me to visit You now. Please forgive me for my sins and for any times I did not fully believe in Your presence in the Blessed Sacrament. Please stay with me.

Mother Mary, please mother me and help me to quiet my mind to focus on your Son, Jesus.

Spiritual Communion, Our Father, Hail Mary, Glory Be, and Prayer to Our Lady of the Most Blessed Sacrament.

Ask Jesus to speak to your heart. Be quiet and listen. If your mind wanders to other things, bring it back by asking Jesus and Mary to help you focus on your prayers. Also ask your guardian angel to assist you.

Praise: O Sacrament Most Holy, O Sacrament Divine, all praise and all thanksgiving be every moment Thine!

Pray: Pray for me, O Virgin Immaculate, Our Lady of the Most Blessed Sacrament.

Savor

Rest in the presence of the Lord. Close your eyes and put yourself into a scene with St. Joseph, Mary, and Jesus in Mary's womb.

Ask Jesus to touch your heart in a special way, according to His holy will. Express your love to Jesus. Stay for as long as you can to keep our Eucharistic Lord company, as your circumstances allow.

Even after you leave your time of Adoration to go on with your responsibilities, recall the scenes and sentiments of your prayer time and any insights you might have gained. Allow your heart to be a living tabernacle and commune with Jesus throughout your day. Feel free to record your thoughts and experiences below.

Lights, insights, resolutions:

_____

_____

_____

_____

_____

_____

Striving to Be a Vessel Like Mary

During this Eucharistic visit, pray for the
graces to be a vessel like Mary.

Ponder

The greatest love story of all time is contained in a tiny white Host.[17]

—Venerable Archbishop Fulton J. Sheen

Reflect

Mother Mary was and is a vessel of grace for all of her children.
In the Litany of Loreto, Mary is described as a "spiritual vessel," a
"vessel of honor," and a "singular vessel of devotion."

St. John Paul II stated: "Mary also anticipated, in the mystery
of the Incarnation, the Church's Eucharistic faith. When, at the
Visitation, she bore in her womb the Word made flesh, she became ... the first 'tabernacle' in history in which the Son of God,
still invisible to our human gaze, allowed himself to be adored by

---

[17] Quoted on the website Archbishop Fulton Sheen, https://celebrate
sheen.com/.

Elizabeth, radiating his light as it were through the eyes and the voice of Mary."[18]

We certainly can't do what Mary has done or is doing still. Yet we can ask for her graces to be able to respond with love to those people in our midst—our family members, our neighbors, co-workers, and complete strangers. We can pray to be a holy vessel of love to those who are hurting or feeling abandoned and unloved for some reason. Adoring Jesus in the Blessed Sacrament will immensely aid us.

Pray

Put yourself in the presence of God. Invite the Blessed Mother to be with you in prayer.

Pray: Dear Jesus, Miracle of the Eucharist, thank You for the great gift of You! And thank You for allowing me to visit You now. Please forgive me for my sins and for any times I did not fully believe in Your presence in the Blessed Sacrament. Please stay with me.

Dear Mary, please grant many graces to me and help me to quiet my mind to focus on your Son, Jesus.

Spiritual Communion, Our Father, Hail Mary, Glory Be, and Prayer to Our Lady of the Most Blessed Sacrament.

Ask Jesus to speak to your heart. Be quiet and listen. If your mind wanders to other things, bring it back by asking Jesus and Mary to help you focus on your prayers. Also ask your guardian angel to assist you.

[18] Pope St. John Paul II, encyclical *Ecclesia de Eucharistia* (April 17, 2003), no. 55.

Praise: O Sacrament Most Holy, O Sacrament Divine, all praise and all thanksgiving be every moment Thine!

Pray: Pray for me, O Virgin Immaculate, Our Lady of the Most Blessed Sacrament.

Savor

Rest in the presence of the Lord. Close your eyes and put yourself into a scene with the Blessed Virgin Mary during any time of her life, responding in love to people in her midst. Prayerfully imagine her with you now.

Ask Jesus to touch your heart in a special way, according to His holy will. Express your love to Jesus. Stay for as long as you can to keep our Eucharistic Lord company, as your circumstances allow.

Even after you leave your time of Adoration to go on with your responsibilities, recall the scenes and sentiments of your prayer time and any insights you might have gained. Allow your heart to be a living tabernacle and commune with Jesus throughout your day. Feel free to record your thoughts and experiences below.

Lights, insights, resolutions:

_____

_____

_____

_____

_____

30 Marian Eucharistic Visits

_____

_____

_____

_____

_____

_____

_____

_____

_____

_____

_____

_____

_____

18

Learning to Be Quiet with Mary

During this Eucharistic visit, pray for the graces to learn to be quiet in order to listen to Our Lord speaking to your heart.

Ponder

Know also that you will probably gain more by praying fifteen minutes before the Blessed Sacrament than by all the other spiritual exercises of the day. True, Our Lord hears our prayers anywhere, for He has made the promise "Ask, and you shall receive," but He has revealed to His servants that those who visit Him in the Blessed Sacrament will obtain a more abundant measure of grace.[19]

—St. Alphonsus Liguori

Reflect

So many of the saints have preached on the importance of spending time with our Eucharistic Lord. St. Alphonsus Liguori emphasized how beneficial time with Our Lord is. St. Faustina spent endless hours with Jesus in the Blessed Sacrament. She wrote in her *Diary*, "O Jesus, concealed in the Blessed Sacrament of the Altar, my only

[19] "Quotes on the Most Blessed Sacrament," 15.

love and mercy, I commend to You all the needs of my body and soul. You can help me, because You are Mercy itself. In You lies all my hope."[20] St. Faustina learned to trust Jesus wholeheartedly with every single thing. She knew she could count on Him to help her with all her needs.

Meek and gentle Mother Mary teaches us silence in prayer with Jesus during our Eucharistic visits. While we are there before Him, we can ask Mary to help us to be quiet in order to listen to our Lord's whispers to our heart.

Pray

Put yourself in the presence of God. Invite the Blessed Mother to be with you in prayer.

Pray: Dear Jesus, Miracle of the Eucharist, thank You for the great gift of You! And thank You for allowing me to visit You now. Please forgive me for my sins and for any times I did not fully believe in Your presence in the Blessed Sacrament. Please stay with me.

Mother Mary, inspire me to be prayerfully silent and open to the whispers of the Holy Spirit. Please help me to quiet my mind to focus on your Son, Jesus.

Spiritual Communion, Our Father, Hail Mary, Glory Be, and Prayer to Our Lady of the Most Blessed Sacrament.

Ask Jesus to speak to your heart. Be quiet and listen. If your mind wanders to other things, bring it back by asking Jesus and Mary to help you focus on your prayers. Also ask your guardian angel to assist you.

[20] St. Maria Faustina Kowalska, *Diary*, 1751.

Praise: O Sacrament Most Holy, O Sacrament Divine, all praise and all thanksgiving be every moment Thine!

Pray: Pray for me, O Virgin Immaculate, Our Lady of the Most Blessed Sacrament.

Savor

Rest in the presence of the Lord. Close your eyes and put yourself into a scene with the Blessed Mother praying quietly at home in Nazareth beside her sleeping Baby Jesus.

Ask Jesus to touch your heart in a special way, according to His holy will. Express your love to Jesus. Stay for as long as you can to keep our Eucharistic Lord company, as your circumstances allow.

Even after you leave your time of Adoration to go on with your responsibilities, recall the scenes and sentiments of your prayer time and any insights you might have gained. Allow your heart to be a living tabernacle and commune with Jesus throughout your day. Feel free to record your thoughts and experiences below.

Lights, insights, resolutions:

_____

_____

_____

_____

_____

19

Learning Obedience with Mary

During this Eucharistic visit, pray for the
graces to be obedient like Mary.

Ponder

*The body given up for us and made present under sacramental
signs was the same body which she had conceived in her womb!*

—Pope St. John Paul II, *Ecclesia de Eucharistia*, no. 56

Reflect

Obedience is often difficult, as it means that we must humble ourselves. Being obedient to God's holy will, however, is a must! Adam
and Eve have shown us the result of disobedience. Our Blessed
Mother was always obedient to the laws, rules, and customs of her
people. How blessed we are that Mother Mary's beautiful obedience
ushered Our Lord and Savior Jesus Christ into the world. Mary
was given a choice, and she chose to cooperate with God's plan.

She and St. Joseph had to be obedient in making a long journey
to Bethlehem. And because of Emperor Caesar Augustus's decree,
Jesus was born in the City of David. Mary remained obedient to the

religious practices at the time, even though she was born without sin. When she and St. Joseph presented Jesus in the temple, they offered the customary temple sacrifice as a purification and expiation of sin. Mary's entire life was marked with signs of obedience.

Can we even imagine Mary's ultimate obedience in giving up her Son to be tortured and crucified?

Pray

Put yourself in the presence of God. Invite the Blessed Mother to be with you in prayer.

Pray: Dear Jesus, Miracle of the Eucharist, thank You for the great gift of You! And thank You for allowing me to visit You now. Please forgive me for my sins and for any times I did not fully believe in Your presence in the Blessed Sacrament. Please stay with me.

Mother Mary, teach me obedience. Please help me to quiet my mind to focus on your Son, Jesus.

Spiritual Communion, Our Father, Hail Mary, Glory Be, and Prayer to Our Lady of the Most Blessed Sacrament.

Ask Jesus to speak to your heart. Be quiet and listen. If your mind wanders to other things, bring it back by asking Jesus and Mary to help you focus on your prayers. Also ask your guardian angel to assist you.

Praise: O Sacrament Most Holy, O Sacrament Divine, all praise and all thanksgiving be every moment Thine!

Pray: Pray for me, O Virgin Immaculate, Our Lady of the Most Blessed Sacrament.

Savor

Rest in the presence of the Lord. Close your eyes and put yourself into the scene with Mary and St. Joseph presenting Jesus in the temple.

Ask Jesus to touch your heart in a special way, according to His holy will. Express your love to Jesus. Stay for as long as you can to keep our Eucharistic Lord company, as your circumstances allow.

Even after you leave your time of Adoration to go on with your responsibilities, recall the scenes and sentiments of your prayer time and any insights you might have gained. Allow your heart to be a living tabernacle and commune with Jesus throughout your day. Feel free to record your thoughts and experiences below.

Lights, insights, resolutions:

_____

_____

_____

_____

_____

_____

_____

_____

_____

_____

_____

_____

_____

_____

_____

_____

_____

_____

_____

20

Learning to Sacrifice with Mary

During this Eucharistic visit, pray for graces to make the necessary sacrifices God asks of you.

Ponder

From the Eucharist comes strength to live the Christian life and zeal to share that life with others.[21]

—Pope St. John Paul II

Reflect

Making sacrifices is often difficult. Yet to offer penance or make a sacrifice for someone else is beneficial not only for that person but for our own souls too. God calls us to be merciful people and help those in need.

Mother Mary led a very sacrificial life. Her life was not her own. She obtained much strength to do her works of mercy from the presence of her Lord Jesus. St. John Paul II tells us that we gain

---

[21] "Quotes on the Most Blessed Sacrament," 3, Real Presence Eucharistic Education and Adoration Association, http://thereal presence.org/eucharst/tes/quotes3.html

strength from the Eucharist to live the Christian life and zeal to share it with others. St. Mother Teresa, who was very devoted to the Mother of God, often preached that she and her Missionaries of Charity Sisters needed to receive Jesus' broken Body in the Eucharist every morning at Holy Mass in order to receive the strength so necessary to go out and take care of the broken bodies of the poor.

Most likely, we will not be doing the work of Mother Teresa —pulling maggots out of the bodies of poor souls left for dead in the gutter, rescuing abandoned babies, and so forth. Yet the Eucharist is essential in our lives too. We absolutely need the strength from Jesus in the Eucharist in order to lead good Christian lives, to be shining lights for others. Our time in Adoration of Our Lord hidden in the tabernacle or exposed in the monstrance will immensely aid our journeys.

Pray

Put yourself in the presence of God. Invite the Blessed Mother to be with you in prayer.

Pray: Dear Jesus, Miracle of the Eucharist, thank You for the great gift of You! And thank You for allowing me to visit You now. Please forgive me for my sins and for any times I did not fully believe in Your presence in the Blessed Sacrament. Please stay with me.

Dear Blessed Mother, teach me to be more generous and sacrificial with my works of mercy for others. Please help me to quiet my mind to focus on your Son, Jesus.

Spiritual Communion, Our Father, Hail Mary, Glory Be, and Prayer to Our Lady of the Most Blessed Sacrament.

Ask Jesus to speak to your heart. Be quiet and listen. If your mind wanders to other things, bring it back by asking Jesus and Mary to help you focus on your prayers. Also ask your guardian angel to assist you.

Praise: O Sacrament Most Holy, O Sacrament Divine, all praise and all thanksgiving be every moment Thine!

Pray: Pray for me, O Virgin Immaculate, Our Lady of the Most Blessed Sacrament.

Savor

Rest in the presence of the Lord. Close your eyes and put yourself into the scene with Mary when she meets her Son on the way to Calvary. Once beloved, He has now been betrayed, arrested, mocked, and tortured. Now she sees Him carrying His Cross and cannot stop what is happening and about to happen. Her heart breaks, but she has consented to this profound sacrifice.

Ask Jesus to touch your heart in a special way, according to His holy will. Express your love to Jesus. Stay for as long as you can to keep our Eucharistic Lord company, as your circumstances allow.

Even after you leave your time of Adoration to go on with your responsibilities, recall the scenes and sentiments of your prayer time and any insights you might have gained. Allow your heart to be a living tabernacle and commune with Jesus throughout your day. Feel free to record your thoughts and experiences below.

Lights, insights, resolutions:

_____

_____

_____

_____

_____

_____

_____

_____

_____

_____

_____

_____

_____

_____

_____

21

Welcoming the Word of God with Mary

During this Eucharistic visit, pray for the graces
always to welcome God's Word into your heart.

Ponder

*The Holy Eucharist is a mystery of faith, which goes beyond our
capacity to understand and requires that we trust completely in the
Word of Christ. Mary teaches us to grow in the theological virtue of
faith. Her disposition of faith, which we are called to imitate, is perhaps
best expressed in the Gospels in her words to the wine stewards at the
Wedding Feast of Cana: "Do whatever He tells you" (John 2:5).*[22]

—Raymond Leo Cardinal Burke

Reflect

The Blessed Virgin Mary held the Word of God in her very womb!
Mary was always obedient to God and believed in the Word of God
at the Annunciation. She pondered God's Word in her heart. As

---

[22] His Eminence Raymond Leo Cardinal Burke, D.D., J.C.D., Commentary on *Ecclesia de Eucharistia*, Marian Catechist Apostolate,
https://www.mariancatechist.com/commentary-on-ecclesia-de
-eucharistia/.

Jesus' Mother, she became, in a sense, His first disciple. Mary is an awesome teacher for us in the spiritual life!

After instituting the Eucharist at the Last Supper, Jesus told His disciples, "Do this in memory of me." We believe through faith that the Holy Eucharist is the Body, Blood, Soul, and Divinity of our dear Savior, Jesus Christ. According to His Eminence Raymond Leo Cardinal Burke, "Mary teaches us to grow in the theological virtue of faith." The theological virtue of faith, which was gifted to us at Baptism, is meant to grow in our hearts.

We will never fully understand the full mystery of the Holy Eucharist until we get to Heaven. Right now, however, we can continually pray for an increase in faith and ask our Mother Mary to help us. We can frequent the Sacrament of the Holy Eucharist, make Spiritual Communions, and adore Jesus in the Blessed Sacrament whenever we are able.

Pray

Put yourself in the presence of God. Invite the Blessed Mother to be with you in prayer.

Pray: Dear Jesus, Miracle of the Eucharist, thank You for the great gift of You! And thank You for allowing me to visit You now. Please forgive me for my sins and for any times I did not fully believe in Your presence in the Blessed Sacrament. Please stay with me.

Blessed Mother Mary, help me to grow in faith and increase my faith. Please help me to quiet my mind to focus on your Son, Jesus.

Spiritual Communion, Our Father, Hail Mary, Glory Be, and Prayer to Our Lady of the Most Blessed Sacrament.

Ask Jesus to speak to your heart. Be quiet and listen. If your mind wanders to other things, bring it back by asking Jesus and Mary to help you focus on your prayers. Also ask your guardian angel to assist you.

Praise: O Sacrament Most Holy, O Sacrament Divine, all praise and all thanksgiving be every moment Thine!

Pray: Pray for me, O Virgin Immaculate, Our Lady of the Most Blessed Sacrament.

Savor

Rest in the presence of the Lord. Close your eyes and put yourself into the scene with Mary at the wedding feast at Cana telling the wine stewards, "Do whatever He tells you."

Ask Jesus to touch your heart in a special way according to His holy will. Express your love to Jesus. Stay for as long as you can to keep our Eucharistic Lord company, as your circumstances allow.

Even after you leave your time of Adoration to go on with your responsibilities, recall the scenes and sentiments of your prayer time and any insights you might have gained. Allow your heart to be a living tabernacle and commune with Jesus throughout your day. Feel free to record your thoughts and experiences below.

Lights, insights, resolutions:

_____

_____

_____

_____

_____

_____

_____

_____

_____

_____

_____

_____

_____

_____

_____

_____

22

Praising God with Mary

During this Eucharistic visit, pray for the
graces to praise God more worthily.

Ponder

*The time you spend with Jesus in the Blessed Sacrament is the
best time that you will spend on earth. Each moment that you
spend with Jesus will deepen your union with Him and make
your soul everlastingly more glorious and beautiful in heaven,
and will help bring about an everlasting peace on earth.*[23]

—St. Teresa of Calcutta

Reflect

Mother Mary's life was a continual exclamation of praise for God.
Her every word, thought, and action brought glory to God, upon
Whom she unceasingly focused. Mary adored and praised God
in carrying out the holy mission entrusted to her. She did so not
only in obediently conceiving of the Holy Spirit, carrying Jesus
in her womb for nine months, giving birth to Him, and lovingly

[23] "Quotes on the Most Blessed Sacrament," 15.

raising Him along with St. Joseph but also in following her Son to His death on the Cross and assisting and uplifting His disciples by her holy presence as they waited for the Holy Spirit to come at Pentecost. We can honestly say that every cell of Mary's being praised and glorified God.

Mary can show us how to praise and glorify God in our own lives. Spending time with Jesus in the Blessed Sacrament with Mary at our side is indeed a perfect place to learn from our Mother Mary.

Pray

Put yourself in the presence of God. Invite the Blessed Mother to be with you in prayer.

Pray: Dear Jesus, Miracle of the Eucharist, thank You for the great gift of You! And thank You for allowing me to visit You now. Please forgive me for my sins and for any times I did not fully believe in Your presence in the Blessed Sacrament. Please stay with me.

Dear Mother Mary, help me to praise God more lovingly. Please help me to quiet my mind to focus on your Son, Jesus.

Spiritual Communion, Our Father, Hail Mary, Glory Be, and *Prayer to Our Lady of the Most Blessed Sacrament.*

Ask Jesus to speak to your heart. Be quiet and listen. If your mind wanders to other things, bring it back by asking Jesus and Mary to help you focus on your prayers. Also ask your guardian angel to assist you.

Praise: O Sacrament Most Holy, O Sacrament Divine, all praise and all thanksgiving be every moment Thine!

Pray: Pray for me, O Virgin Immaculate, Our Lady of the Most Blessed Sacrament.

Savor

Rest in the presence of the Lord. Close your eyes and put yourself into the scene with Mary assisting the disciples — her very presence bringing comfort to them and allaying their fears.

Ask Jesus to touch your heart in a special way, according to His holy will. Express your love to Jesus. Stay for as long as you can to keep our Eucharistic Lord company, as your circumstances allow.

Even after you leave your time of Adoration to go on with your responsibilities, recall the scenes and sentiments of your prayer time and any insights you might have gained. Allow your heart to be a living tabernacle and commune with Jesus throughout your day. Feel free to record your thoughts and experiences below.

Lights, insights, resolutions:

_____

_____

_____

_____

_____

_____

_____

23

Drawing Closer to God with Mary

During this Eucharistic visit, pray for the graces
to be more present to God in your prayers.

Ponder

*The Eucharist had so powerful an attraction for the Blessed
Virgin that she could not live away from it. She lived in it
and by it. She passed her days and her nights at the feet of
her divine Son.... Her love for her hidden God shone in her
countenance and communicated its ardour to all about her.*[24]

—St. Peter Julian Eymard

Reflect

Our Mother Mary lived in the presence of Jesus. She was completely
permeated with Him. Yes, Jesus was her Son, but He was also, and
importantly, her Redeemer and Savior—the King of Kings and
Lord of Lords. Mary was acutely attentive to every single teaching
from her Son, both silent and verbal.

---

[24] "Quotes on the Most Blessed Sacrament," 15.

St. John Eudes wrote about Mary's pondering in her heart. He said, "In that Heart she kept all the mysteries, marvels and every event of the life of her beloved Son, our Redeemer, to be the object of her love and of all the sentiments, aspirations and affections of her soul."[25]

After Jesus had been crucified and had risen from the dead, Mary would commune with Him each time she received Him in the Eucharist.

Pray

Put yourself in the presence of God. Invite the Blessed Mother to be with you in prayer.

Pray: Dear Jesus, Miracle of the Eucharist, thank You for the great gift of You! And thank You for allowing me to visit You now. Please forgive me for my sins and for any times I did not fully believe in Your presence in the Blessed Sacrament. Please stay with me.

Dear Mother Mary, please draw me closer to your Son, Jesus, and help me to quiet my mind to focus on your Him.

Spiritual Communion, Our Father, Hail Mary, Glory Be, and Prayer to Our Lady of the Most Blessed Sacrament.

Ask Jesus to speak to your heart. Be quiet and listen. If your mind wanders to other things, bring it back by asking Jesus and Mary to help you focus on your prayers. Also ask your guardian angel to assist you.

---

[25] St. John Eudes, *The Admirable Heart of Mary*, pt. 6, chap. 4.

Praise: O Sacrament Most Holy, O Sacrament Divine, all praise and all thanksgiving be every moment Thine!

Pray: Pray for me, O Virgin Immaculate, Our Lady of the Most Blessed Sacrament.

Savor

Rest in the presence of the Lord. Close your eyes and put yourself into the scene with Mary united to her Son Jesus in Holy Communion.

Ask Jesus to touch your heart in a special way, according to His holy will. Express your love to Jesus. Stay for as long as you can to keep our Eucharistic Lord company, as your circumstances allow.

Even after you leave your time of Adoration to go on with your responsibilities, recall the scenes and sentiments of your prayer time and any insights you might have gained. Allow your heart to be a living tabernacle and commune with Jesus throughout your day. Feel free to record your thoughts and experiences below.

Lights, insights, resolutions:

_____

_____

_____

_____

_____

24

Treasuring and Pondering with Mary

During this Eucharistic visit, pray for the graces
to learn from the treasury of Mary's heart as
she brings you ever closer to Jesus.

Ponder

*At the moment of the Incarnation, Mary anticipated
what happens for us faithful at every Eucharist: Christ
becomes present for us, under the species of bread and wine,
so that we may receive Him into our very being.*[26]

—Raymond Leo Cardinal Burke

Reflect

Scripture tells us, "But Mary treasured all these words and pondered them in her heart." (Luke 2:19). St. John Eudes wrote extensively on Mary's pondering words and deeds in her heart. He wrote, "Mary kept all these things in her Heart, that is, all the marvelous events of our Savior's life. 'This holy Virgin,' writes St.

[26] Burke, Commentary on *Ecclesia de Eucharistia*.

Ambrose, 'always carried in the depths of her heart the mysteries of God and the Passion of her Son and whatever else He did.'"

St. John Eudes eloquently described all the reasons and ways in which Mary kept all sacred things in her heart. He explained, "Our Lady knew that no part of the Savior's life could be termed small, that everything in Him was great, divine and admirable and that each one of His footsteps, each breath, each flutter of his eyelids, each very least thought of His, deserved the eternal adoration of angels and men." Therefore, as the saint explained, Mary's eyes were "constantly fixed on her beloved Son, and she was ever vigilant and attentive to the smallest detail of His life." Mary "kept them as medicine to heal our souls from all types of evil and as a powerful remedy to fill mankind with all kinds of good."[27]

Pray

Put yourself in the presence of God. Invite the Blessed Mother to be with you in prayer.

Pray: Dear Jesus, Miracle of the Eucharist, thank You for the great gift of You! And thank You for allowing me to visit You now. Please forgive me for my sins and for any times I did not fully believe in Your presence in the Blessed Sacrament. Please stay with me.

Dear Mother Mary, please share your treasures with me and help me to quiet my mind to focus on your Son, Jesus.

Spiritual Communion, Our Father, Hail Mary, Glory Be, and Prayer to Our Lady of the Most Blessed Sacrament.

---

[27] St. John Eudes, *The Admirable Heart of Mary*, pt. 6, chap. 4.

Ask Jesus to speak to your heart. Be quiet and listen. If your mind wanders to other things, bring it back by asking Jesus and Mary to help you focus on your prayers. Also ask your guardian angel to assist you.

Praise: O Sacrament Most Holy, O Sacrament Divine, all praise and all thanksgiving be every moment Thine!

Pray: Pray for me, O Virgin Immaculate, Our Lady of the Most Blessed Sacrament.

Savor

Rest in the presence of the Lord. Close your eyes and put yourself into a scene with Mary lovingly observing her Son and treasuring Him and His actions in her heart.

Ask Jesus to touch your heart in a special way, according to His holy will. Express your love to Jesus. Stay for as long as you can to keep our Eucharistic Lord company, as your circumstances allow.

Even after you leave your time of Adoration to go on with your responsibilities, recall the scenes and sentiments of your prayer time and any insights you might have gained. Allow your heart to be a living tabernacle and commune with Jesus throughout your day. Feel free to record your thoughts and experiences below.

Lights, insights, resolutions:

_____

_____

_____

_____

_____

_____

_____

_____

_____

_____

_____

_____

_____

25

Learning Chastity with Mary

During this Eucharistic visit, pray for the graces to
lead a chaste life according to your state in life.

Ponder

*Reflecting upon the relationship between Mary's faith at the
Annunciation and Birth of our Lord, and our faith in the
Holy Eucharist, we are inspired to express ever deeper devotion
and love every time we are blessed to be in the presence of
the Blessed Sacrament or to receive Holy Communion.*[28]

—Raymond Leo Cardinal Burke

Reflect

The Blessed Virgin Mary inspires us to a deeper faith and belief in
the Real Presence of Jesus in the Blessed Sacrament. Each time we
are blessed to be near Jesus in the Blessed Sacrament or to receive
Him in the Eucharist should be yet another beautiful and blessed
opportunity to grow deeper in our faith. Mary's deep faith and

---

[28] Burke, Commentary on *Ecclesia de Eucharistia.*

virtuous, chaste life should prod us to strive for holiness. We will never be as holy as the Blessed Virgin Mary, yet we can pray to emulate her virtues.

The virtue of chastity is essential for everyone in every state of life. The *Catechism* instructs: "The virtue of chastity comes under the cardinal virtue of *temperance*, which seeks to permeate the passions and appetites of the senses with reason." Further it states: "All the baptized are called to chastity. The Christian has 'put on Christ,' the model for all chastity. All Christ's faithful are called to lead a chaste life in keeping with their particular states of life. At the moment of his Baptism, the Christian is pledged to lead his affective life in chastity" (nos. 2341, 2348).

Let us ask Mary to guide us in true chastity.

Pray

Put yourself in the presence of God. Invite the Blessed Mother to be with you in prayer.

Pray: Dear Jesus, Miracle of the Eucharist, thank You for the great gift of You! And thank You for allowing me to visit You now. Please forgive me for my sins and for any times I did not fully believe in Your presence in the Blessed Sacrament. Please stay with me.

Dear Mother Mary, please guide me in true chastity and help me to quiet my mind to focus on your Son, Jesus.

Spiritual Communion, Our Father, Hail Mary, Glory Be, and Prayer to Our Lady of the Most Blessed Sacrament.

Ask Jesus to speak to your heart. Be quiet and listen. If your mind wanders to other things, bring it back by asking Jesus and

Mary to help you focus on your prayers. Also ask your guardian angel to assist you.

Praise: O Sacrament Most Holy, O Sacrament Divine, all praise and all thanksgiving be every moment Thine!

Pray: Pray for me, O Virgin Immaculate, Our Lady of the Most Blessed Sacrament.

Savor

Rest in the presence of the Lord. Close your eyes and put yourself into the scene with Mary at the birth of Our Lord Jesus in Bethlehem.

Ask Jesus to touch your heart in a special way according to His holy will. Express your love to Jesus. Stay for as long as you can to keep our Eucharistic Lord company, as your circumstances allow.

Even after you leave your time of Adoration to go on with your responsibilities, recall the scenes and sentiments of your prayer time and any insights you might have gained. Allow your heart to be a living tabernacle and commune with Jesus throughout your day. Feel free to record your thoughts and experiences below.

Lights, insights, resolutions:

_____

_____

_____

_____

_____

_____

_____

_____

_____

_____

_____

_____

_____

_____

_____

_____

_____

26

Allowing God to Use Us with Mary

During this Eucharistic visit, pray for the graces to be more present to God and open to doing His holy will.

Ponder

Whenever I go to the chapel, I put myself in the presence of our good Lord, and I say to Him, "Lord, I am here. Tell me what You would have me to do." ... And then, I tell God everything that is in my heart. I tell Him about my pains and my joys, and then I listen. If you listen, God will also speak to you, for with the good Lord, you have to both speak and listen. God always speaks to you when you approach Him plainly and simply.[29]

—St. Catherine Labouré

Reflect

The saints have told us that time with Our Lord is precious and comforting. St. Catherine Labouré had a very close relationship with the Blessed Mother. On November 27, 1830, the Blessed Mother appeared to St. Catherine in the chapel of her convent

---

[29] "Quotes on the Most Blessed Sacrament," 15.

in Paris, France, and entrusted her with the task of making the Miraculous Medal. This humble saint always let Our Lord know that she was there at His feet, ready and willing to do His holy will. She poured her heart out to Jesus but always made sure she quieted down in order to hear Him speak to her heart and soul. In our verse today, she assures us that God will speak to us when we approach Him "plainly and simply."

Mother Teresa once gave me a little prayer card. On one side, it said: "The fruit of silence is prayer; the fruit of prayer is faith; the fruit of faith is love; the fruit of love is service, the fruit of service is peace." It starts with prayer blossoming from silence. Let's be quiet and let God speak to our hearts. From our conversations with Jesus will blossom faith, love, service, and peace.

Pray

Put yourself in the presence of God. Invite the Blessed Mother to be with you in prayer.

Pray: Dear Jesus, Miracle of the Eucharist, thank You for the great gift of You! And thank You for allowing me to visit You now. Please forgive me for my sins and for any times I did not fully believe in Your presence in the Blessed Sacrament. Please stay with me.

Mother Mary, please guide me to your Son and help me to quiet my mind to focus on Him.

Spiritual Communion, Our Father, Hail Mary, Glory Be, and Prayer to Our Lady of the Most Blessed Sacrament.

Ask Jesus to speak to your heart. Be quiet and listen. If your mind wanders to other things, bring it back by asking Jesus and

Mary to help you focus on your prayers. Also ask your guardian angel to assist you.

> *Praise*: O Sacrament Most Holy, O Sacrament Divine, all praise and all thanksgiving be every moment Thine!
>
> *Pray*: Pray for me, O Virgin Immaculate, Our Lady of the Most Blessed Sacrament.

Savor

Rest in the presence of the Lord. Close your eyes in your time of Adoration and put yourself into the scene with Mother Mary and St. Catherine in Paris, France.

Ask Jesus to touch your heart in a special way according to His holy will. Express your love to Jesus. Stay for as long as you can to keep our Eucharistic Lord company, as your circumstances allow.

Even after you leave your time of Adoration to go on with your responsibilities, recall the scenes and sentiments of your prayer time and any insights you might have gained. Allow your heart to be a living tabernacle and commune with Jesus throughout your day. Feel free to record your thoughts and experiences below.

Lights, insights, resolutions:

_____

_____

_____

_____

27

Learning with Mary That Nothing Is Impossible with God

During this Eucharistic visit, pray for the graces
to learn from the Blessed Virgin Mary.

Ponder

O King of glory, though You hide Your beauty, yet the eye of my soul
rends the veil. I see the angelic choirs giving You honor without cease.

—St. Maria Faustina Kowalska, *Diary*, 80

Reflect

When the Virgin Mary heard the angel Gabriel's greeting at the Annunciation, she was in complete awe and then in total acceptance of God's holy will. When Mary asked the angel Gabriel, "How can this be?" he explained, "Nothing will be impossible for God" (Luke 1:34, 37). Mary knew that if she agreed, there might very well be huge consequences ahead for her, especially because she was a virgin and others would have a lot of trouble understanding this amazing miracle—being pregnant before her marriage to St. Joseph. Yet Mary faithfully and courageously submitted herself completely to God's will that she would conceive by the Holy Spirit and give birth to the world's Redeemer. Holy Mary responded, "Here am I, the servant of the Lord; let it be with me according to your word" (Luke 1:38).

Let us surrender our lives in complete confidence, asking Mother Mary to be at our side. Time with Jesus in the Blessed Sacrament, adoring Him and listening to Him, will transform our hearts and souls. After all, nothing is impossible for God!

Pray

Put yourself in the presence of God. Invite the Blessed Mother to be with you in prayer.

Pray: Dear Jesus, Miracle of the Eucharist, thank You for the great gift of You! And thank You for allowing me to visit You now. Please forgive me for my sins and for any times I did not fully believe in Your presence in the Blessed Sacrament. Please stay with me.

My Mother Mary, please pray for me and help me to quiet my mind to focus on your Son, Jesus.

Spiritual Communion, Our Father, Hail Mary, Glory Be, and Prayer to Our Lady of the Most Blessed Sacrament.

Ask Jesus to speak to your heart. Be quiet and listen. If your mind wanders to other things, bring it back by asking Jesus and Mary to help you focus on your prayers. Also ask your guardian angel to assist you.

Praise: O Sacrament Most Holy, O Sacrament Divine, all praise and all thanksgiving be every moment Thine!

Pray: Pray for me, O Virgin Immaculate, Our Lady of the Most Blessed Sacrament.

Savor

Rest in the presence of the Lord. Close your eyes and put yourself into the scene of the Annunciation with young Mary and the angel Gabriel.

Ask Jesus to touch your heart in a special way according to His holy will. Express your love to Jesus. Stay for as long as you can to keep our Eucharistic Lord company, as your circumstances allow.

Even after you leave your time of Adoration to go on with your responsibilities, recall the scenes and sentiments of your prayer time and any insights you might have gained. Allow your heart to be a living tabernacle and commune with Jesus throughout your day. Feel free to record your thoughts and experiences below.

Lights, insights, resolutions:

_____

_____

_____

_____

_____

_____

_____

_____

_____

_____

_____

_____

_____

_____

_____

_____

_____

_____

_____

_____

28

Allowing Mary to Come to Our Aid

During this Eucharistic visit, pray for the
graces to stay close to Jesus and Mary.

Ponder

*The Holy Father reminds us that all that Christ accomplished for
us on Calvary is made present for us in the Holy Mass. This is
the meaning of His words: "Do this in remembrance of me" (Luke
22:9) (no. 57a). Therefore, at every Eucharist, Christ once again
gives Mary to us as our Mother and gives us to her as her true sons
and daughters, as He did when He died on the cross for us.*[30]

—Raymond Leo Cardinal Burke

Reflect

Our Blessed Mother is with us at every Holy Communion we receive and at every visit to her Son in the Blessed Sacrament. Jesus
and Mary are inseparable. We should always invite Mary to come
with us to every Holy Mass and help us to worship. Jesus gave us

---

[30] Burke, Commentary on *Ecclesia de Eucharistia*.

the unfathomable gift of His own Mother as He hung on the Cross for our salvation. Certainly, Jesus desires that His Mother guide us to Heaven. She will always come to our aid.

Mother Teresa, who loved the Blessed Mother very much, came to my rescue during a precarious pregnancy. I had previously lost three babies to miscarriage and later had to be on complete bedrest for almost an entire pregnancy due to a hemorrhage in my uterus and a heart condition. The doctor told me I was losing the baby. I knew Mother Teresa at the time and got word to her about my situation. She wrote to me and sent me a blessed Miraculous Medal. She encouraged me to trust that the Blessed Mother would help me. Among other recommendations, she said to pray, "Mary, Mother of Jesus, be Mother to me now." Very simple but powerful. Thanks be to God, my baby survived, and so did I! I named my newborn daughter after Mother Mary and her mother, St. Anne.

Pray

Put yourself in the presence of God. Invite the Blessed Mother to be with you in prayer.

Pray: Dear Jesus, Miracle of the Eucharist, thank You for the great gift of You! And thank You for allowing me to visit You now. Please forgive me for my sins and for any times I did not fully believe in Your presence in the Blessed Sacrament. Please stay with me.

Mary, Mother of Jesus, be Mother to me now. Please help me to quiet my mind to focus on your Son, Jesus.

Spiritual Communion, Our Father, Hail Mary, Glory Be, and Prayer to Our Lady of the Most Blessed Sacrament.

Ask Jesus to speak to your heart. Be quiet and listen. If your mind wanders to other things, bring it back by asking Jesus and Mary to help you focus on your prayers. Also ask your guardian angel to assist you.

Praise: O Sacrament Most Holy, O Sacrament Divine, all praise and all thanksgiving be every moment Thine!

Pray: Pray for me, O Virgin Immaculate, Our Lady of the Most Blessed Sacrament.

Savor

Rest in the presence of the Lord. Close your eyes and put yourself into the scene with Jesus on the Cross, dying for your salvation and giving you personally the great gift of His Holy Mother.

Ask Jesus to touch your heart in a special way, according to His holy will. Express your love to Jesus. Stay for as long as you can to keep our Eucharistic Lord company, as your circumstances allow.

Even after you leave your time of Adoration to go on with your responsibilities, recall the scenes and sentiments of your prayer time and any insights you might have gained. Allow your heart to be a living tabernacle and commune with Jesus throughout your day. Feel free to record your thoughts and experiences below.

Lights, insights, resolutions:

_____

_____

_____

_____

_____

_____

_____

_____

_____

_____

_____

_____

_____

_____

_____

29

Adoring Jesus While Praying for Mary's Graces

During this Eucharistic visit, pray for the graces to
adore Jesus more earnestly and more often.

Ponder

*Mary shows her maternal care of us by urging us to go to Christ,
to put our faith in Him, to trust in His words spoken at the
Last Supper, that is to believe that the Eucharistic species of the
bread and wine are, in truth, the Body and Blood of Christ.*[31]

—Raymond Leo Cardinal Burke

Reflect

The Blessed Virgin Mary is the Mediatrix of grace. Mary actively
consented to and cooperated in her Son's redemptive act, making her Co-Redemptrix (meaning *with* Him, not equal to Him, in
redemption). Mary's role continues in the distribution of graces.
St. Bernardine of Siena stated, "Every grace that is communicated
to this world has a threefold course. For by excellent order, it is

---

[31] Burke, Commentary on *Ecclesia de Eucharistia*.

121

dispensed from God to Christ, from Christ to the Virgin, from the Virgin to us."[32]

In the vision of her proposed Miraculous Medal, rays of graces streamed from the rings on the Blessed Mother's fingers when she appeared to St. Catherine Labouré on November 27, 1830. St. Catherine noticed that not every ring produced the brilliant, beautiful rays of light. The Blessed Mother explained: "These rays symbolize the graces I shed upon those who ask for them. The gems from which rays do not fall are the graces for which souls forget to ask." The graces are available but must be requested of Mary. We need to ask her for as many graces as we can receive!

Pray

Put yourself in the presence of God. Invite the Blessed Mother to be with you in prayer.

Pray: Dear Jesus, Miracle of the Eucharist, thank You for the great gift of You! And thank You for allowing me to visit You now. Please forgive me for my sins and for any times I did not fully believe in Your presence in the Blessed Sacrament. Please stay with me.

Please, dear Blessed Mother, grant many graces to me and help me to quiet my mind to focus on your Son, Jesus.

Spiritual Communion, Our Father, Hail Mary, Glory Be, and Prayer to Our Lady of the Most Blessed Sacrament.

Ask Jesus to speak to your heart. Be quiet and listen. If your mind wanders to other things, bring it back by asking Jesus and

---

[32] Sermon on the Nativity of the Blessed Virgin Mary, no. 6.

Mary to help you focus on your prayers. Also ask your guardian angel to assist you.

Praise: O Sacrament Most Holy, O Sacrament Divine, all praise and all thanksgiving be every moment Thine!

Pray: Pray for me, O Virgin Immaculate, Our Lady of the Most Blessed Sacrament.

Savor

Rest in the presence of the Lord. Close your eyes and put yourself into the scene with Mary with rays of grace extending from her rings, as she appeared to St. Catherine Labouré.

Ask Jesus to touch your heart in a special way, according to His holy will. Express your love to Jesus. Stay for as long as you can to keep our Eucharistic Lord company, as your circumstances allow.

Even after you leave your time of Adoration to go on with your responsibilities, recall the scenes and sentiments of your prayer time and any insights you might have gained. Allow your heart to be a living tabernacle and commune with Jesus throughout your day. Feel free to record your thoughts and experiences below.

Lights, insights, resolutions:

_____

_____

_____

_____

_____

_____

_____

_____

_____

_____

_____

_____

_____

_____

_____

_____

_____

30

Asking Mary to Be Our Mother

During this Eucharistic visit, pray for the
graces to be lovingly devoted to Mary.

Ponder

*I adore You, Lord and Creator, hidden in the Most Blessed
Sacrament. I adore You for all the works of Your hands, that reveal
to me so much wisdom, goodness and mercy, O Lord. You have
spread so much beauty over the earth and it tells me about Your
beauty, even though these beautiful things are but a faint reflection
of You, incomprehensible Beauty. And although You have hidden
Yourself and concealed your beauty, my eye, enlightened by faith,
reaches You and my souls recognizes its Creator, its Highest Good,
and my heart is completely immersed in prayer of adoration.*

—St. Maria Faustina Kowalska, *Diary*, 1692

Reflect

We can only imagine the wondrous simple and poignant moments
between Mary and her Son, Jesus, as she and St. Joseph raised Him
in their humble home in Nazareth. Every moment was magnificently

holy as Mary cared for her Son, as any loving mother would do, but also as she adored Him profoundly because He was also the Savior of the world. We might experience a glimpse of this unfathomable beauty in Heaven one day.

For now, we can ask Mary to be our Mother, too, and to assist us in our adoration of her Son. We can ask her to give us the graces we need and to guide us ever closer to her Son's magnificent Sacred Heart.

Pray

Put yourself in the presence of God. Invite the Blessed Mother to be with you in prayer.

Pray: Dear Jesus, Miracle of the Eucharist, thank You for the great gift of You! And thank You for allowing me to visit You now. Please forgive me for my sins and for any times I did not fully believe in Your presence in the Blessed Sacrament. Please stay with me.

Mother Mary, be my Mother forever. Please help me to quiet my mind to focus on your Son, Jesus.

Spiritual Communion, Our Father, Hail Mary, Glory Be, and Prayer to Our Lady of the Most Blessed Sacrament.

Ask Jesus to speak to your heart. Be quiet and listen. If your mind wanders to other things, bring it back by asking Jesus and Mary to help you focus on your prayers. Also ask your guardian angel to assist you.

Praise: O Sacrament Most Holy, O Sacrament Divine, all praise and all thanksgiving be every moment Thine!

Pray: Pray for me, O Virgin Immaculate, Our Lady of the Most Blessed Sacrament.

Savor

Rest in the presence of the Lord. Close your eyes and put yourself into a scene with Mary as a young mother with her Son, Jesus.

Ask Jesus to touch your heart in a special way, according to His holy will. Express your love to Jesus. Stay for as long as you can to keep our Eucharistic Lord company, as your circumstances allow.

Even after you leave your time of Adoration to go on with your responsibilities, recall the scenes and sentiments of your prayer time and any insights you might have gained. Allow your heart to be a living tabernacle and commune with Jesus throughout your day. Feel free to record your thoughts and experiences below.

Lights, insights, resolutions:

_____

_____

_____

_____

_____

_____

_____

_____

_____

_____

_____

_____

_____

_____

_____

_____

_____

May Mary, Mother of the Redeemer,
continue to draw me ever closer to her Divine Son.

Afterword

Do we have faith the size of a ... no, not a mustard seed. Do we have faith the size of a second grader's faith? One of my second-grade religion students exclaimed something deeply profound to me one day. It was during my lesson on the Eucharist when young Felicia opened her heart to me. She got up out of her seat and hurried to the front of the classroom. She was bursting to tell me. She then whispered in my ear, "I believe. But I want to believe *more!*" This innocent child was entirely serious. And her passion was not lost on me.

I share this precious experience with you because I think we can all learn from an innocent child to desire and to possess that childlike faith and to endeavor to grow in our faith! We can pray for it! Faith is a virtue we were given at Baptism, and it is like a muscle that is meant to be used — meant to grow in our hearts. We can ask Our Lord for an increase in Faith!

We can also learn from a more seasoned member of the Church. He told us, "The Church draws her life from the Eucharist." Pope St. John Paul II opened his Encyclical Letter *Ecclesia de Eucharistia* with these straightforward yet powerful words. In this letter, the pontiff had so much to say about Jesus, our Eucharistic Lord. I encourage you to read it in its entirety and be inspired.

St. John Paul II also gives us direction and great encouragement:

In the humble signs of bread and wine, changed into his body and blood, Christ walks beside us as our strength and our food for the journey, and he enables us to become, for everyone, witnesses of hope. If, in the presence of this mystery, reason experiences its limits, the heart, enlightened by the grace of the Holy Spirit, clearly sees the response that is demanded, and bows low in adoration and unbounded love. (no. 62)

Let us lovingly visit our Eucharistic Lord often and seek His presence beside us "as our strength and our food for the journey." Right beside Jesus, and with a childlike and ever-growing faith, we can become great witnesses of hope to a weary world, stirring the fading embers into brilliant roaring flames of faith! Onward!

May God bless you in great abundance!

Your sister in Christ,
Donna-Marie Cooper O'Boyle
May 2, 2023
Birthday of St. Catherine Labouré

Prayers

The *Catechism* gives a succinct definition of prayer as a "vital and personal relationship with the living and true God" (2558). Prayer is a "covenant relationship between God and man in Christ," and it is Christian "insofar as it is communion with Christ" (2565, 2564).

Countless saints have defined prayer or have given their advice on prayer. St. Teresa of Ávila, for example, stated that we compliment God when we pray, and she described prayer as a close sharing between friends. St. Thérèse of Lisieux said, "For me, prayer is a surge of the heart; it is a simple look, turned toward heaven, it is a cry of recognition and of love, embracing both trial and joy."[33] St. Teresa of Calcutta often preached the necessity of retreating to the silence of our hearts so that we can hear God speak to us. She said that listening to God is the beginning of prayer. St. John Vianney said, "Prayer is the inner bath of love into which the soul plunges itself." St. Francis de Sales was famous for preaching the need for daily prayer and said that when we are extra busy, we need to pray more!

---

[33] *Manuscrits Autobiographiques*, C 25rr, cited in CCC 2558.

St. Peter Julian Eymard gives very practical advice: "As far as possible, you should pray in quiet and silent devotion. Try to have a favorite topic of prayer, such as a devotion to the Passion of Jesus, the Blessed Sacrament, awareness of the divine presence; go directly to Jesus without too much fuss." He also said, "Have confidence in prayer. It is the unfailing power which God has given us. By means of it you will obtain the salvation of the dear souls whom God has given you and all your loved ones. 'Ask and you shall receive,' Our Lord said. Be yourself with the good Lord."[34]

Act of Spiritual Communion
by St. Alphonsus de Liguori

My Jesus, I believe that Thou art truly present in the Most Blessed Sacrament. I love Thee above all things and I desire to possess Thee within my soul. Since I am unable now to receive Thee sacramentally, come at least spiritually into my heart. I embrace Thee as being already there, and unite myself wholly to Thee; never, never permit me to be separated from Thee.

Jesus, my sweet love, wound, inflame this heart of mine, so that it may be always and all on fire for Thee.

Divine Praises

Blessed be God.
Blessed be His holy name.
Blessed be Jesus Christ, true God and true man.
Blessed be the Name of Jesus.

---

[34] "Quotations from the Writings of Saint Peter Julian Eymard," Congregation of the Blessed Sacrament, https://blessedsacrament. com/us/st-peter-julian-eymard/quotes-st-peter-julian-eymard/.

Blessed be His Most Sacred Heart.
Blessed be His Most Precious Blood.
Blessed be Jesus in the Most Holy Sacrament of the Altar.
Blessed be the Holy Spirit, the Paraclete.
Blessed be the great Mother of God, Mary most holy.
Blessed be her holy and Immaculate Conception.
Blessed be her glorious Assumption.
Blessed be the name of Mary, Virgin and Mother.
Blessed be Saint Joseph, her most chaste spouse.
Blessed be God in His angels and in His saints. Amen.

Prayer to Our Lady of the Most Blessed Sacrament
by St. Peter Julian Eymard

O Virgin Mary, Our Lady of the Most Blessed Sacrament, the glory of Christians, the joy of the universal Church, and the hope of the world, pray for us. Kindle in all the faithful a lively devotion to the most Holy Eucharist, so that they may all be made worthy to receive Holy Communion every day. Our Lady of the Most Blessed Sacrament, pray for us. Let us with Mary Immaculate adore, thank, supplicate, and console the most Sacred and beloved Eucharistic Heart of Jesus!

Angel's Prayer at Fátima

Most Holy Trinity; Father, Son, and Holy Spirit—I adore Thee profoundly. I offer Thee the most precious Body, Blood, Soul and Divinity of Jesus Christ, present in all the tabernacles of the world, in reparation for the outrages, sacrileges, and indifferences whereby He is offended. And through the infinite merits of His Most Sacred Heart and the Immaculate Heart of Mary, I beg of Thee the conversion of poor sinners.

A Short Visit to the Blessed Sacrament
before Meditation
by Saint John Henry Newman

Make the Sign of the Cross. Then pray:

I place myself in the presence of Him, in whose incarnate presence I am before I place myself there. I adore Thee, O my Savior, present here as God and man, in Soul and Body, in true Flesh and Blood.

I acknowledge and confess that I kneel before that Sacred Humanity, which was conceived in Mary's womb and lay in Mary's bosom; which grew up to man's estate and by the Sea of Galilee called the Twelve, wrought miracles, and spoke words of wisdom and peace; which in due season hung on the Cross, lay in the tomb, rose from the dead, and now reigns in Heaven.

I praise, and bless, and give myself wholly to Him, who is the true Bread of my soul and my everlasting joy.

Litany of the Most Blessed Sacrament
by St. Peter Julian Eymard

Lord, have mercy. *Lord, have mercy.*
Christ, have mercy. *Christ, have mercy.*
Lord, have mercy. *Lord, have mercy.*
Christ, hear us. Christ, *graciously hear us.*
God the Father of Heaven, *have mercy on us.*
God the Son, Redeemer of the world ...
God the Holy Spirit ...
Holy Trinity, one God ...
Jesus, Eternal High Priest of the Eucharistic Sacrifice ...
Jesus, Divine Victim on the Altar for Our Salvation ...
Jesus, hidden under the Appearance of Bread ...

Jesus, dwelling in the Tabernacles of the world …
Jesus, really, truly, and substantially present in the
    Blessed Sacrament …
Jesus, abiding in your fulness, Body, Blood, Soul, and
    Divinity …
Jesus, Bread of Life …
Jesus, Bread of Angels …
Jesus, with us always until the end of the world …
Sacred Host, summit and source of all worship and
    Christian life …
Sacred Host, sign and cause of the Unity of the Church …
Sacred Host, adored by countless angels …
Sacred Host, spiritual food …
Sacred Host, Sacrament of Love …
Sacred Host, bond of charity …
Sacred Host, greatest aid to holiness …
Sacred Host, gift and glory of the priesthood …
Sacred Host, in which we partake of Christ …
Sacred Host, in which the soul is filled with grace …
Sacred Host, in which we are given a pledge of future
    glory …
Blessed be Jesus in the Most Holy Sacrament of the Altar.
Blessed be Jesus in the Most Holy Sacrament of the Altar.
Blessed be Jesus in the Most Holy Sacrament of the Altar.
For those who do not believe in Your Eucharistic Presence,
    have mercy, O Lord.
For those who are indifferent to the Sacrament of Your
    love, *have mercy on us.*
For those who have offended You in the Holy Sacrament
    of the Altar, *have mercy on us.*

That we may show fitting reverence when entering Your
holy temple, *we beseech You, hear us.*

That we may make suitable preparation before approach-
ing the altar ...

That we may receive You frequently in Holy Communion
with real devotion and true humility ...

That we may never neglect to thank You for so wonderful
a blessing ...

That we may cherish time spent in silent prayer before
You ...

That we may grow in knowledge of this Sacrament of
sacraments ...

That all priests may have a profound love of the Holy
Eucharist ...

That they may celebrate the Holy Sacrifice of the Mass in
accordance with its sublime dignity ...

That we may be comforted and sanctified with Holy
Viaticum at the hour of our death ...

That we may see You one day face-to-face in Heaven ...

Lamb of God, You take away the sins of the world,
spare us, O Lord.

Lamb of God, You take away the sins of the world,
graciously hear us, O Lord.

Lamb of God, You take away the sins of the world,
have mercy on us, O Lord.

V. O Sacrament most holy, O Sacrament divine,

R. All praise and all thanksgiving be every moment
Thine.

Let us pray. Most merciful Father, You continue to draw
us to Yourself through the Eucharistic mystery. Grant us

fervent faith in this Sacrament of Love, in which Christ the Lord Himself is contained, offered, and received. We make this prayer through the same Christ Our Lord. Amen.

Litany of the Holy Eucharist

Lord, have mercy. *Lord, have mercy.*

Christ, have mercy. *Christ, have mercy.*

Lord, have mercy. *Lord, have mercy.*

Jesus, the Most High, *have mercy on us.*

Jesus, the holy One …

Jesus, Word of God …

Jesus, only Son of the Father …

Jesus, Son of Mary …

Jesus, crucified for us …

Jesus, risen from the dead …

Jesus, reigning in glory …

Jesus, coming in glory …

Jesus, our Lord …

Jesus, our hope …

Jesus, our peace …

Jesus, our Savior …

Jesus, our salvation …

Jesus, our resurrection …

Jesus, Judge of all …

Jesus, Lord of the Church …

Jesus, Lord of creation …

Jesus, Lover of all …

Jesus, life of the world …

Jesus, freedom for the imprisoned …

Jesus, joy of the sorrowing …

Jesus, giver of the Spirit ...

Jesus, giver of good gifts ...

Jesus, source of new life ...

Jesus, Lord of life ...

Jesus, eternal High Priest ...

Jesus, Priest and Victim ...

Jesus, true Shepherd ...

Jesus, true Light ...

Jesus, Bread of Heaven ...

Jesus, Bread of life ...

Jesus, Bread of thanksgiving ...

Jesus, life-giving Bread ...

Jesus, Holy Manna ...

Jesus, New Covenant ...

Jesus, food for everlasting life ...

Jesus, food for our journey ...

Jesus, holy banquet ...

Jesus, true sacrifice ...

Jesus, perfect sacrifice ...

Jesus, eternal sacrifice ...

Jesus, Divine Victim ...

Jesus, Mediator of the New Covenant ...

Jesus, mystery of the altar ...

Jesus, medicine of immortality ...

Jesus, pledge of eternal glory ...

Jesus, Lamb of God, You take away the sins of the world ...

Jesus, Bearer of our sins, You take away the sins of the
world ...

Jesus, Redeemer of the world, You take away the sins of
the world ...

Christ, hear us. *Christ, hear us.*

Christ, graciously hear us. *Christ, graciously hear us.*
Lord Jesus, hear our prayer. *Lord Jesus, hear our prayer.*

Litany of the Most Precious Blood

Lord, have mercy. *Lord, have mercy.*
Christ, have mercy. *Christ, have mercy.*
Lord, have mercy. *Lord, have mercy.*
God our Father in Heaven, *have mercy on us.*
God the Son, Redeemer of the world, *have mercy on us.*
God the Holy Spirit, *have mercy on us.*
Holy Trinity, one God, *have mercy on us.*
Blood of Christ, only Son of the Father, *be our salvation.*
Blood of Christ, Incarnate Word ...
Blood of Christ, the new and eternal covenant ...
Blood of Christ, that spilled to the ground ...
Blood of Christ, that flowed at the scourging ...
Blood of Christ, dripping from the thorns ...
Blood of Christ, shed on the Cross ...
Blood of Christ, the price of our redemption ...
Blood of Christ, our only claim to pardon ...
Blood of Christ, our blessing cup ...
Blood of Christ, in which we are washed ...
Blood of Christ, torrent of mercy ...
Blood of Christ, which overcomes evil ...
Blood of Christ, strength of the martyrs ...
Blood of Christ, endurance of the saints ...
Blood of Christ, that makes the barren fruitful ...
Blood of Christ, protection of the threatened ...
Blood of Christ, comfort of the weary ...
Blood of Christ, solace of the mourner ...
Blood of Christ, hope of the repentant ...

Blood of Christ, consolation of the dying ...
Blood of Christ, our peace and refreshment ...
Blood of Christ, our pledge of life ...
Blood of Christ, by which we pass to glory ...
Blood of Christ, most worthy of honor ...
Lamb of God, You take away the sins of the world, *have mercy on us.*
Lamb of God, You take away the sins of the world, *have mercy on us.*
Lamb of God, You take away the sins of the world, *have mercy on us.*
Lord, You redeemed us by Your blood. *You have made us a Kingdom to serve our God.*

Let us pray. Father, by the blood of Your Son, You have set us free and saved us from death. Continue Your work of love within us, that by constantly celebrating the mystery of our salvation, we may reach the eternal life it promises. We ask this through Christ Our Lord. Amen.

Blessed Sacrament Chaplet

This chaplet is prayed using a string of thirty-three beads with a medal of the Blessed Sacrament. It recalls the thirty-three years of Christ's life on earth.

On the medal, make a Spiritual Communion as follows:

As I cannot now receive Thee, my Jesus, in Holy Communion, come spiritually into my heart and make it Thine own forever.

On each bead, say:

Jesus in the Blessed Sacrament, have mercy on us!

Hail to Thee, True Body
(a prayer to our Eucharistic Lord)

Hail to Thee, true Body born
From Virgin Mary's womb!
The same that on the Cross was nailed
And bore for man the bitter doom.
Thou, Whose side was pierced and flowed
Both with water and with blood;
Suffer us to taste of Thee,
In our life's last agony.
O kind, O loving One!
O sweet Jesus, Mary's Son!

Anima Christi

Soul of Christ, sanctify me.
Body of Christ, save me.
Blood of Christ, inebriate me.
Water from the side of Christ, wash me.
Passion of Christ, strengthen me.
O good Jesus, hear me.
Within Your wounds conceal me.
Do not permit me to be parted from You.
From the evil foe protect me.
At the hour of my death call me.
And bid me come to You,
to praise You with all your saints
forever and ever. Amen.

Memorare

Remember, O most gracious Virgin Mary, that never was it known that anyone who fled to thy protection, implored thy help, or sought thine intercession was left unaided. Inspired by this confidence, I fly unto thee, O Virgin of virgins, my Mother; to thee do I come, before thee I stand, sinful and sorrowful. O Mother of the Word Incarnate, despise not my petitions, but in thy mercy hear and answer me. Amen.

St. Alphonsus Liguori's Prayer for a Visit to the Blessed Sacrament

My Lord Jesus Christ, Who for the love which You bear us, remain night and day in this Sacrament full of compassion and love, awaiting, calling, and welcoming all who come to visit You, I believe that You are present in the Sacrament of the Altar. I adore You from the abyss of my nothingness, and I thank You for all the graces which You have bestowed upon me and in particular for having given me Yourself in this Sacrament, for having given me Your most holy Mother Mary as my Advocate, and for having called me to visit You in this church.

I now salute Your most loving Heart; and this for three ends: first, in thanksgiving for this great gift; secondly, to make amends to You for all the outrages which You receive in this Sacrament from all Your enemies; thirdly, I intend by this visit to adore You in all the places on earth in which You are present in this Sacrament and in which You are the least reserved and the most abandoned. My Jesus, I love You with all my heart. I grieve for having hitherto so many times offended Your infinite goodness. I purpose, by Your grace, nevermore to offend You for the time to come.

And now, miserable and unworthy though I be, I consecrate myself to You without reserve; I give You and renounce my entire will, affections, my desires, and all that I possess. Henceforward, dispose of me and of all that I have as You please. All that I ask of You and desire is Your holy love, final perseverance, and the perfect accomplishment of Your will. I recommend to You the souls in Purgatory, and especially those who had the greatest devotion to the Most Blessed Sacrament, and to the most Blessed Virgin Mary. I also recommend to You all poor sinners.

Finally, my dear Savior, I unite all my affections with the affections of Your most loving Heart, and I offer them, thus united, to Your Eternal Father, and beseech Him in Your name to vouchsafe for Your love, to accept and grant them. Amen.

Chaplet of the Divine Mercy

St. Faustina was given this prayer chaplet by Our Lord. Pray it using rosary beads.

Make the Sign of the Cross.

Our Father
Hail Mary
Apostles' Creed

On the large beads, pray:

Eternal Father, I offer You the Body and Blood, Soul and Divinity of Your dearly beloved Son, Our Lord Jesus Christ, in atonement for our sins and those of the whole world.

On the small beads, pray:

V: For the sake of His sorrowful passion,
R: Have mercy on us and on the whole world.

At the end of the five decades, repeat three times:

Holy God, Holy Mighty One, Holy Immortal One, have mercy on us and on the whole world.

St. Faustina's Litany to the Blessed Host

O Blessed Host, in golden chalice enclosed for me,
That through the vast wilderness of exile I may
    pass—pure, immaculate, undefiled;
Oh, grant that through the power of Your love
This might come to be.
O Blessed Host, take up Your dwelling within my soul,
O Thou my heart's purest love!
With Your brilliance the darkness dispel.
Refuse not Your grace to a humble heart.
O Blessed Host, enchantment of all heaven,
Though Your beauty be veiled
And captured in a crumb of bread,
Strong faith tears away that veil. (*Diary*, 159)

Litany of the Most Sacred Heart of Jesus

Lord, have mercy. *Lord, have mercy.*
Christ, have mercy. *Christ, have mercy.*
Lord, have mercy. *Lord, have mercy.*
Christ, hear us. *Christ, hear us.*
Christ, graciously hear us. *Christ, graciously hear us.*
God, our Father in Heaven, *have mercy on us.*
God the Son, Redeemer of the world, *have mercy on us.*
God, the Holy Spirit, *have mercy on us.*
Holy Trinity, One God, *have mercy on us.*
Heart of Jesus, Son of the Eternal Father, *have mercy on us.*

Heart of Jesus, formed by the Holy Spirit in the womb of
the Virgin Mary ...

Heart of Jesus, united in substance to the Word of God ...

Heart of Jesus, of infinite majesty ...

Heart of Jesus, sacred temple of God ...

Heart of Jesus, tabernacle of the Most High One ...

Heart of Jesus, house of God and gate of Heaven ...

Heart of Jesus, burning furnace of charity ...

Heart of Jesus, abode of justice and love ...

Heart of Jesus, full of goodness and love ...

Heart of Jesus, wellspring of all virtues ...

Heart of Jesus, most worthy of all praise ...

Heart of Jesus, king and center of all hearts ...

Heart of Jesus, in whom are all the treasures of wisdom
and knowledge ...

Heart of Jesus, in whom dwells the fullness of divinity ...

Heart of Jesus, in whom the Father was well pleased ...

Heart of Jesus, of whose fullness we have all received ...

Heart of Jesus, desire of the everlasting hills ...

Heart of Jesus, patient and most merciful ...

Heart of Jesus, enriching all who invoke You ...

Heart of Jesus, fountain of life and holiness ...

Heart of Jesus, atonement for our sins ...

Heart of Jesus, overwhelmed with insults ...

Heart of Jesus, bruised for our offenses ...

Heart of Jesus, obedient unto death ...

Heart of Jesus, pierced with a lance ...

Heart of Jesus, source of all consolation ...

Heart of Jesus, our life and resurrection ...

Heart of Jesus, our peace and reconciliation ...

Heart of Jesus, victim of sins ...

Heart of Jesus, salvation of those who trust in You ...
Heart of Jesus, hope of those who die in You ...
Heart of Jesus, delight of all the saints ...
Lamb of God, You take away the sins of the world,
    spare us, O Lord.
Lamb of God, You take away the sins of the world,
    graciously hear us, O Lord.
Lamb of God, You take away the sins of the world,
    have mercy on us, O Lord.
Jesus, meek and humble of heart, *make our hearts*
    like to Yours.

Let us pray. God our loving Father, grant wisdom to those who govern us, compassion and courage to those who work to defend human life, and safety and care to every human being. For You alone, who formed us in our mothers' wombs, and who call us home to Heaven, are God, for ever and ever. Amen.

Prayer to the Eucharistic Heart of Jesus

Heart of Jesus in the Eucharist, I adore You.
    Sweet Companion of our exile, I seek You.
    Holy God become man, I beat with Your Heart.
Eucharistic Heart of Jesus,
    solitary, abandoned,
    humiliated, cursed,
    despised, outraged,
    ignored by men,
    have mercy on us.
Lover of our hearts,
    pleading for Your beloved,
    patiently waiting for us,

eager to hear our confidences,

desirous of our devotion,

have mercy on us.

Heart of grace,

silent and wishing to speak,

Refuge of the hidden life,

Sharer of the secrets of union with God,

Eucharistic Heart of Jesus,

have mercy on us.

Jesus, Victim, I want to comfort You.

I unite myself with You.

I offer myself in union with You.

I count myself as nothing before You.

I desire to forget myself and think only of You,

to be forgotten and rejected for love of You,

not to be understood, not to be loved, except by You.

I will hold my peace that I may listen to You.

I will forsake myself in order to be lost in You.

Grant that I may quench Your thirst for my salvation,

Your burning thirst for my sanctification,

and that, being purged, I may give You a true and

pure love.

I no longer want to deny Your expectations.

Take me. I give myself to You.

I entrust to You all my actions and thoughts—

my mind, that You may enlighten it,

my heart, that You may fill it,

my will, that You may establish it,

my soul and body, that You may feed and sustain them.

Eucharistic Heart of Jesus,

Whose Blood is the life of my soul,

may it no longer be I who live,
but You alone who lives in me.

Stay with Us
by Pope St. John Paul II

Stay with us today, and stay from now on, every day, according to the desire of my heart, which accepts the appeal of so many hearts from various parts, sometimes far away.... Stay that we may meet You in prayers of adoration and thanksgiving, in prayers of expiation and petition to which all those who visit this basilica are invited.... May the unworthy successor of Peter and all those who take part in the adoration of Your Eucharistic Presence attest with every visit and make ring out again the truth contained in the Apostle's words: "Lord, you know everything. You know that I love you." Amen.[35]

Litany to the Holy Spirit

Lord, have mercy on us.
Lord, have mercy on us.
Lord, have mercy on us.
God the Father of Heaven, *have mercy on us.*
God the Son, Redeemer of the world, *have mercy on us.*
God the Holy Spirit, *have mercy on us.*
Holy Trinity, One God, *have mercy on us.*
Divine Essence, one true God, *have mercy on us.*

---

[35] From a prayer following Mass and exposition of the Blessed Sacrament on December 2, 1981, on the occasion of Pope St. John Paul II's inauguration of perpetual Adoration in the Blessed Sacrament Chapel of St. Peter's Basilica. *L'Osservatore Romano*, December 14, 1981.

Spirit of truth and wisdom ...

Spirit of holiness and justice ...

Spirit of understanding and counsel ...

Spirit of love and joy ...

Spirit of peace and patience ...

Spirit of longanimity and meekness ...

Spirit of benignity and goodness ...

Love substantial of the Father and the Son ...

Love and life of saintly souls ...

Fire ever burning ...

Living water to quench the thirst of hearts ...

From all evil ...

From all impurity of soul and body ...

From all gluttony and sensuality ...

From all attachments to the things of the earth ...

From all hypocrisy and pretense ...

From all imperfections and deliberate faults ...

From our own will ...

From slander ...

From deceiving our neighbors ...

From our passions and disorderly appetites ...

From our inattentiveness to Thy holy inspirations ...

From despising little things ...

From debauchery and malice ...

From love of comfort and luxury ...

From wishing to seek or desire anything other than Thee ...

From everything that displeases Thee ...

Most loving Father, *forgive us.*

Divine Word, *have pity on us.*

Holy and divine Spirit, *leave us not until we are in possession of the Divine Essence, Heaven of heavens.*

Lamb of God, Who takest away the sins of the world, *send us the divine Consoler.*

Lamb of God, Who takest away the sins of the world, *fill us with the gifts of Thy Spirit.*

Lamb of God, Who takest away the sins of the world, *make the fruits of the Holy Spirit increase within us.*

V. Come, O Holy Spirit, fill the hearts of Thy faithful,

R. *And enkindle in them the fire of Thy love.*

V. Send forth Thy Spirit, and they shall be created,

R. *And Thou shalt renew the face of the earth.*

Let us pray. God, Who by the light of the Holy Spirit instructed the hearts of the faithful, grant us by the same Spirit to be truly wise and ever to rejoice in His consolation. Through Jesus Christ Our Lord. Amen.

Litany for Humility

O Jesus! meek and humble of heart, *hear me.*

From the desire of being esteemed, *deliver me, Jesus.*

From the desire of being loved ...

From the desire of being extolled ...

From the desire of being honored ...

From the desire of being praised ...

From the desire of being preferred to others ...

From the desire of being consulted ...

From the desire of being approved ...

From the fear of being humiliated ...

From the fear of being despised ...

From the fear of suffering rebukes ...

From the fear of being calumniated ...

From the fear of being forgotten ...

From the fear of being ridiculed ...

From the fear of being wronged …
From the fear of being suspected …
That others may be loved more than I,
   Jesus, grant me the grace to desire it.
That others may be esteemed more than I …
That, in the opinion of the world, others may increase
   and I may decrease …
That others may be chosen and I set aside …
That others may be praised and I unnoticed …
That others may be preferred to me in everything …
That others may become holier than I, provided that I
   may become as holy as I should …

Totus Tuus Prayer
by Pope Saint John Paul II

Immaculate Conception, Mary my Mother,
Live in me, act in me;
Speak in me and through me;
Think your thoughts in my mind;
Love through my heart;
Give me your dispositions and feelings;
Teach, lead me, and guide me to Jesus;
Correct, enlighten and expand my thoughts and
   behavior;
Possess my soul;
Take over my entire personality and life, replace it
   with yourself;
Incline me to constant adoration;
Pray in me and through me;
Let me live in you and keep me in this union always.
Amen.

At the Feet of Christ in the Eucharist
by St. Maria Faustina Kowalska

O Jesus, Divine Prisoner of Love, when I consider Your love and how You emptied Yourself for me, my senses deaden. You hide Your inconceivable majesty and lower Yourself to miserable me. O King of Glory, though You hide Your beauty, yet the eye of my soul rends the veil. I see the angelic choirs giving You honor without cease, and all the heavenly powers praising You without cease, and without cease they are saying: Holy, Holy, Holy.

Oh, who will comprehend Your love and Your unfathomable mercy toward us! O Prisoner of Love, I lift up my poor heart in this tabernacle that it may adore You without cease night and day. I know of no obstacle in this adoration: and even though I be physically distant, my heart is always with You. Nothing can put a stop to my love for You. No obstacles exist for me....

O Holy Trinity, one and indivisible God, may You be blessed for this great gift and testament of mercy. Amen. I adore You, Lord and Creator, hidden in the Most Blessed Sacrament. I adore You for all the works of Your hands, that reveal to me so much wisdom, goodness and mercy, O Lord. You have spread so much beauty over the earth and it tells me about Your beauty, even though these beautiful things are but a faint reflection of You, incomprehensible Beauty. And although You have hidden Yourself and concealed your beauty, my eye, enlightened by faith, reaches You and my souls recognizes its Creator, its Highest Good, and my heart is completely immersed in prayer of adoration.

My Lord and Creator, Your goodness encourages me to converse with You. Your mercy abolishes the chasm which separates the Creator from the creature. To converse with You, O Lord, is the delight of my heart. In You I find everything that my heart could desire. Here Your light illumines my mind, enabling it to know You more and more deeply. Here streams of grace flow down upon my heart. Here my soul draws eternal life. O my Lord and Creator, You alone, beyond all these gifts, give Your own self to me and unite Yourself intimately with Your miserable creature.

O Christ, let my greatest delight be to see You loved and Your praise and glory proclaimed, especially the honor of Your mercy. O Christ, let me glorify Your goodness and mercy to the last moment of my life, with every drop of my blood and every beat of my heart. Would that I be transformed into a hymn of adoration of You. When I find myself on my deathbed, may the last beat of my heart be a loving hymn glorifying Your unfathomable mercy. Amen.

Come Then, Good Shepherd

by St. Thomas Aquinas, as quoted in
Pope St. John Paul II's Ecclesia de Eucharistia

Come then, Good Shepherd, bread divine,
Still show to us Thy mercy sign;
Oh, feed us, still keep us Thine;
So we may see Thy glories shine
in fields of immortality.

O Thou, the wisest, mightiest, best,
Our present food, our future rest,
Come, make us each Thy chosen guest,
Co-heirs of Thine, and comrades blest
With saints whose dwelling is with Thee.

Acknowledgments

I am deeply grateful to my parents, Eugene Joseph and Alexandra Mary Cooper, for bringing me into the world and raising me in a large Catholic family. To my brothers and sisters—Alice Jean, Gene, Gary, Barbara, Tim, Michael, and David—thank you for being a wonderful part of my life.

My heartfelt gratitude goes to my husband, Dave, and my beloved children—Justin, Chaldea, Jessica, Joseph, and Mary-Catherine—for their continued love and support, and to my precious grandsons, Shepherd and Leo. I love you all dearly!

Special thanks to my friend Servant of God Father John Hardon, S.J., who has spiritually directed and encouraged me and is no doubt continuing from Heaven! Also, an exuberant thank-you to dear Mother Teresa for playing a huge role in shaping me spiritually and for being a mother to me, which I know she continues even now. And a profound thank-you to my dear friend and spiritual director Fr. Andrew Apostoli, C.F.R., whose loving teachings continue to stir my heart.

I owe special gratitude to EWTN Publishing for asking that I write this book—to Michael P. Warsaw, Taylor Wilson, Devin

Jones, and all of the wonderful EWTN team who helped get this book out to you! It is a special blessing for me to partner with EWTN on this book. The Eternal Word Television Network has held a special place in my heart, beginning with my creating and hosting three television series on the network, as well as having been a grateful guest on many of the shows—both radio and television. May God continue to bless the network and the wonderful hardworking people who keep it going.

I also want to thank my dear Sisters in Christ, United Under Mary's Mantle, for their generous prayers for the ministry. And I cannot forget dear Felicia, whose passion to grow in faith has stirred my heart.

Finally, I am extremely thankful for my readership, viewership, and listenership and to all those I meet along my travels. Thank you for being part of my fascinating journey through life! I pray for you. Please pray for me too. We are all on this journey together—helping one another along the way!

About the Author

Donna-Marie Cooper O'Boyle never planned to become an author, a television host, or an international speaker. Then again, she always desired to help others by sharing the Faith. It all unfolded during a precarious pregnancy, when God put her on complete bed rest. It was during that time of trying to preserve the life of her unborn baby and her own life when Donna-Marie became deeply inspired to begin writing her many books.

Because of God's amazing grace, Donna-Marie is a Catholic wife, a mother of five children, a grandmother of two, and an award-winning and best-selling author and journalist, TV host, international speaker, and pilgrimage and retreat leader. She is the television host of EWTN's *Everyday Blessings for Catholic Moms*, *Catholic Mom's Café*, and *Feeding Your Family's Soul*, which she created to teach, encourage, and inspire Catholic families. Her love for children and imparting the Faith spurred her on to serve as a catechist for more than thirty years. She is an extraordinary minister of the Eucharist at her parish.

Donna-Marie was noted as one of the Top Ten Most Fascinating Catholics in 2009 by *Faith & Family Live*. She enjoyed a decade-long friendship with St. Teresa of Calcutta, became a Lay Missionary of Charity, and started a branch of the Lay Missionaries of Charity for Mother Teresa. For many years, her spiritual director was Servant of God John A. Hardon, S.J., who also served as one of Mother Teresa's spiritual directors.

In 2008, Donna-Marie was invited by the Holy See to participate in an international congress for women at the Vatican to mark the twentieth anniversary of the Apostolic Letter *Mulieris Dignitatem* (*On the Dignity and Vocation of Women*). She received apostolic blessings from Pope Emeritus Benedict XVI for her books and her work and a special blessing from Pope St. John Paul II for her writing on St. Teresa of Calcutta. Donna-Marie has received many awards from the Catholic Press Association, the Connecticut Press Club, and the National Federation of Press Women for her books and was given a Media Award from the American Cancer Society for her volunteer column on cancer victims and survivors.

Donna-Marie is the author of more than thirty-five books on faith, family, and the saints — including her memoir, *The Kiss of Jesus: How Mother Teresa and the Saints Helped Me to Discover the Beauty of the Cross*. She is also a general editor for the Divine Mercy Catholic Bible (Ascension Press, 2020) and has written two major Divine Mercy articles for that Bible.

Donna-Marie's work has been featured in several Catholic magazines, in national newspapers, and on numerous websites and Internet columns. Some of her articles have been featured in *L'Osservatore Romano*, *Magnificat*, *National Catholic Register*, *Catholic World Report*, *Our Sunday Visitor*, and other publications. In addition to her own television shows, Donna-Marie has been profiled on many others, including Fox News, Rome Reports, Vatican Insider, and several programs on EWTN: *Women of Grace*, *EWTN News Nightly*, *Sunday Night Prime*, *EWTN Live*, *The Choices We Face*, *At*

About the Author

Home with Jim and Joy, *The Journey Home*, and *Faith & Culture*. She is a regular guest on national and international radio shows as well and has hosted her own show.

Most of all, Donna-Marie strives to live in the present moments of life, where she discovers many beautiful opportunities to reach out with Christ's love to others. She encourages others to do the same. Donna-Marie lives with her family in rural New England, admiring God's creation, gardening, working on new books, and designing and creating Catholic jewelry and sacramentals.

She lectures throughout the world on topics relating to Catholic and Christian women, faith, and families, the saints, and her friend Mother Teresa. She also writes much on Divine Mercy and is an authority on the life of St. Faustina Kowalska.

Donna-Marie can be reached through her websites, www.donnacooperoboyle.com and www.feedingyourfamilyssoul.com, where you can learn more about her books, ministry, and pilgrimages, and where she also maintains blogs. Follow her on social media and watch her YouTube channel.

Notes

Notes

Notes